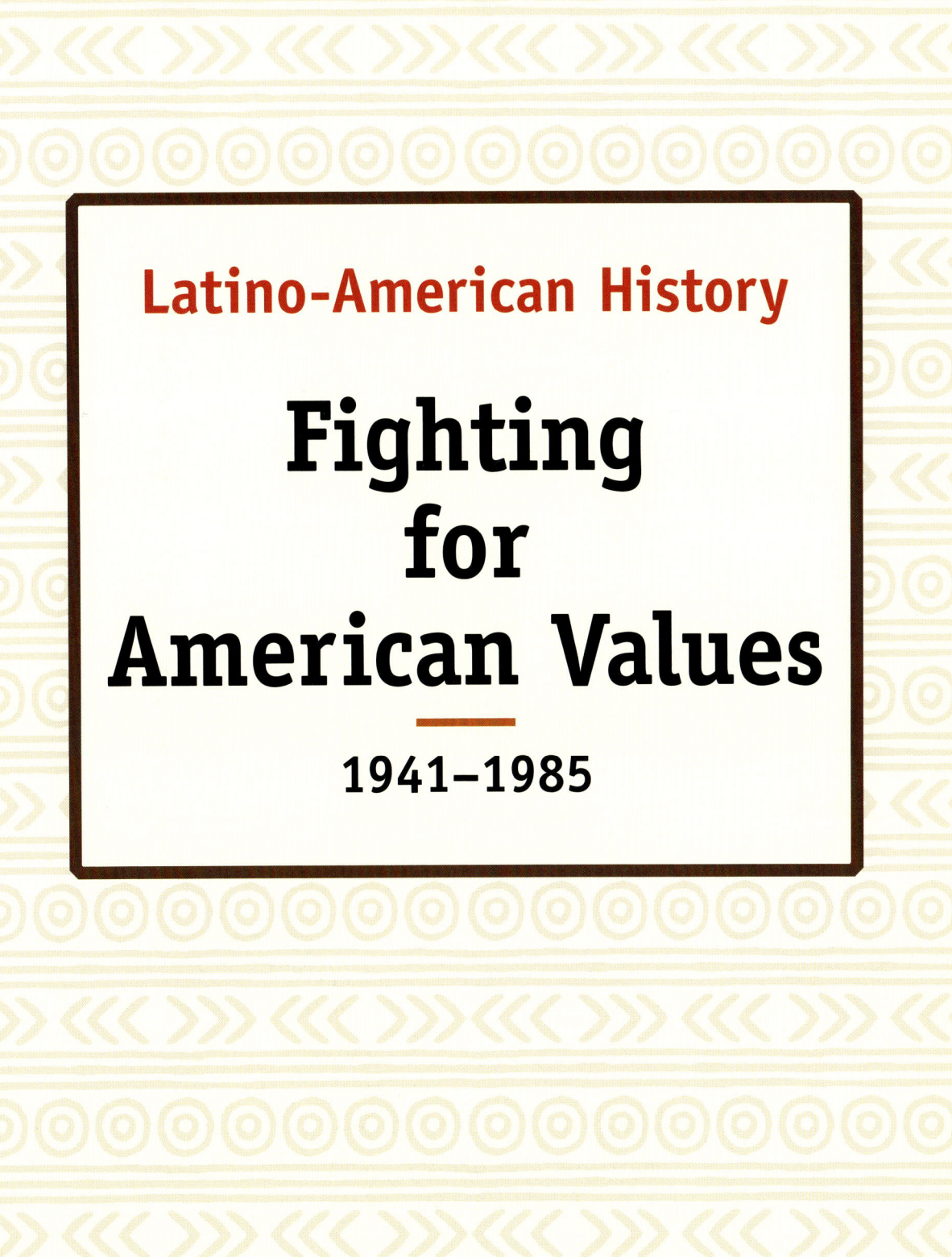

## Latino-American History

# Fighting for American Values

1941–1985

# Latino-American History

## The Spanish Conquest of America
Prehistory to 1775

## Independence for Latino America
1776–1821

## Spanish Settlement in North America
1822–1898

## Struggling to Become American
1899–1940

## Fighting for American Values
1941–1985

## Creating a New Future
1986 to Present

## Latino-American History

# Fighting for American Values

## 1941–1985

by Robin Doak

Mark Overmyer-Velázquez, Ph.D., Consulting Editor

**COVER** *At Fort Benning, in Georgia, in 1943, troops of Mexican descent in a new regiment of infantry receive orders in both Spanish and English.*

**Fighting for American Values**

Copyright ©2007 by Infobase Publishing

All rights reserved. No part of this book may be reproduced or utilized in any form or by any means, electronic or mechanical, including photocopying, recording, or by any information storage or retrieval systems, without permission in writing from the publisher.

For information contact:

Chelsea House
An imprint of Infobase Publishing
132 West 31st Street
New York, NY 10001

**Library of Congress Cataloging-in-Publication Data**
Doak, Robin S. (Robin Santos), 1963-
 Fighting for American values, 1941-1985 / Robin Doak.
   p. cm.. — (Latino-American history)
 Includes bibliographical references and index.
 ISBN 0-8160-6444-X (hardcover)
 1. Hispanic Americans—History—20th century—Juvenile literature. 2. Hispanic Americans—Social conditions—20th century—Juvenile literature. 3. Hispanic Americans—Politics and government—20th century—Juvenile literature. 4. Immigrants—United States—History—20th century—Juvenile literature. 5. Latin America—Emigration and immigration—History—20th century—Juvenile literature. 6. United States—Emigration and immigration—History—20th century—Juvenile literature. 7. United States—Ethnic relations—History—20th century—Juvenile literature. I. Title. II. Series.
 E184.S75D628 2006
 973'.0468—dc22
2006028376

Chelsea House books are available at special discounts when purchased in bulk quantities for businesses, associations, institutions, or sales promotions. Please call our Special Sales Department in New York at (212) 967–8800 or (800) 322–8755.

You can find Chelsea House on the World Wide Web at http://www.chelseahouse.com

Cover design by Takeshi Takehashi

A Creative Media Applications Production
Interior design: Fabia Wargin & Luis Leon
Editor: Matt Levine
Copy editor: Laurie Lieb

**Photo Credits**
© Bettmann/CORBIS page: cover; The Granger Collection, New York, page: vi; New York Public Library, Astor, Lenox and Tilden Foundations pages: 8, 12; © The Dorothea Lange Collection, Oakland Museum of California, City of Oakland, Gift of Paul S. Taylor page: 18; Associated Press pages: 21, 24, 27, 34, 37, 42, 44, 47, 54, 57, 60, 64, 78, 80, 84, 86, 91, 95; Library of Congress pages: 31, 51, 70; Landov page: 74

Maps: Created by Ortelius Design

Printed in the United States of America

Bang CMA 10 9 8 7 6 5 4 3 2 1

This book is printed on acid-free paper.

All links and Web addresses were checked and verified to be correct at the time of publication. Because of the dynamic nature of the Web, some addresses and links may have changed since publication and may no longer be valid.

# Contents

Preface to the Series ................................................. 1

Introduction ......................................................... 9

1  Latinos and World War II ........................................ 13

2  Latinos in Postwar Society ...................................... 25

3  New Latino Arrivals from the Americas ........................... 35

4  The Great Migration from Puerto Rico ............................ 45

5  Latino Immigration from the Caribbean ........................... 55

6  The Struggle for Civil Rights ................................... 65

7  New Political Power ............................................. 75

8  A Growing Cultural Influence .................................... 85

Timeline ............................................................ 98

Glossary ............................................................ 99

Further Reading .................................................... 100

Bibliography ....................................................... 101

Index .............................................................. 102

About the Author ................................................... 106

# Preface to the Series

by Mark Overmyer-Velázquez, Ph.D.,
Consulting Editor

"With all due respect to Uncle Sam, this [march] shows that Los Angeles has never stopped belonging to Mexico." This statement by Alberto Tinoco, a television reporter in Mexico, refers to the demonstration in support of immigrants that took place in Los Angeles, California, on March 25, 2006. An estimated 1 million people attended this march—mainly Mexicans and other Latinos. But does Los Angeles belong to Mexico? And what was so important that so many people came out to show their support for Latino immigrants?

The *Latino American History* series looks to answer these questions and many others. Los Angeles did belong to Mexico until 1848. At that time, Los Angeles and much of what is now called the American Southwest became part of the United States as a result of the Mexican-American War. Today, the enormous city, like many other places throughout the United States, is home to millions of Latinos.

The immigrant march made perfectly clear that people of Latin American descent have a historical power and presence in the United States. Latino history is central to

OPPOSITE   A Mexican farm laborer works in a sugar beet field near Fisher, Minnesota, in 1937. Thousands of Latinos have worked on farms throughout the United States for more than a century.

the history of the United States. Latinos have been closely connected to most regions in the United States in every era, from the 16th-century Spanish settlements in Florida and California to the contemporary surge of Latino populations in North Carolina, South Carolina, Oklahoma, Minnesota, and Connecticut.

The 2000 U.S. Census made Latinos' importance even plainer. Every 10 years, the government makes a survey of the country's population, called a census. The 2000 survey determined that, for the first time, Latinos outnumbered African Americans as the second-largest nonwhite population.

One of every seven people in the nation identifies himself or herself as Latino. This ethnic group has accounted for about half the growth in the U.S. population since 1990. There are over 41 million people of Latin American and Caribbean origins in the United States. Their presence will have a large impact on the futures of both the United States and Latin America.

## Who Is Latino?

The term *Latino* emerged in the 1970s. It refers—somewhat loosely—to people, either male or female, living in the United States who have at least one parent of Latin American descent. The term is often used in contrast to terms such as *Anglo American, African American,* and *Asian American.* Most frequently, *Latino* refers to immigrants (and their descendants) who originally came to the United States from the Spanish-speaking countries of North, Central, and South America, as well as from countries in the

Caribbean. This definition usually does not include Brazil, Haiti, and Belize, where the chief language is not Spanish, but does include Puerto Rico, which is a U.S. territory.

The other popular term to describe this population, *Hispanic,* was developed by the U.S. government in the 1970s as a way to categorize people of Latin American descent. However, Latinos consider this label to wrongly identify them more with Spain than with Latin America. In addition, most Latinos first identify with their own national or subnational (state, city, or village) origins. For example, a woman with roots in the Dominican Republic might first identify herself as *una dominicana* and then as a Latina. The word *Latino* causes further confusion when discussing the thousands of non–Spanish-speaking American Indians who have immigrated to the United States from Latin America.

Four main factors over time have determined the presence of Latinos in the United States. They are U.S. military and economic involvement in Latin America, relaxed immigration laws for entry into the United States, population growth in Latin America, and wages that were higher in the United States than in Latin America. These factors have shaped the patterns of migration to the United States since the mid-19th century.

## "We Didn't Cross the Border, the Border Crossed Us"

### 1848

Many Mexicans still call the Mexican-American War from 1846 to 1848 the "North American Invasion." In the first decades of the 19th century, Mexico's economy and military were weak from years of fighting. There had been a war for independence from Spain followed by a series of civil wars among its own people. During the same period, the United States was eager to expand its borders. It looked to Mexico for new land. The war cost Mexico almost half its territory, including what would become the U.S. states of California, Nevada, Arizona, New Mexico, and Texas. Some Mexican citizens left on the U.S. side of the new border proclaimed, "We didn't cross the border, the border crossed us."

The territory that had belonged to Mexico brought new citizens of Mexican background to the United States, as well as enormous mineral and land wealth. Consider the famous gold rush that started in 1848 on former Mexican territory in California. That event and the vast expanse of farmlands and pasture lands once belonging to Mexico were vital to the westward expansion of the United States. Mexicans on the north side of the new border became U.S. citizens and the country's first Latinos. As the West became industrialized and demand for labor grew, it was often migrant Mexican workers who labored in the fields and factories of the prospering economy.

## 1898

## The Spanish-American War, Puerto Rico, and the Harvest of Empire

The term *harvest of empire* refers to the arrival of Latino immigrants in the United States as a direct result of U.S. military involvement in Latin America, starting with Mexico in 1848. The United States created political and economic uncertainty through the use of force and the support of dictatorships in the "garden" of Latin America. Then the United States harvested the resulting millions of homeless and jobless Latinos. The United States's harvest of empire peaked with the 1898 Spanish-American War.

> **Fast Fact**
>
> American Indians who have migrated to the United States may identify themselves with a small village or perhaps a state of origin. For example, Zapoteco immigrants from the state of Oaxaca, Mexico, have developed Oaxacan hometown associations in Los Angeles and other U.S. cities.

The U.S. military freed the island of Puerto Rico from Spanish colonial rule in 1898. The island's residents never would have imagined that they would be colonized yet again, this time by the United States. The island became a U.S. territory. The U.S. president had the power to choose the governor and other high-level administrators. In 1917, Congress made all Puerto Ricans U.S. citizens.

In the 1950s, Puerto Rico suffered economic problems and joblessness. Immigration to the United States rapidly expanded, resulting in the largest movement of Latin Americans to the United States in history. New laws in the 1960s only increased Latin American immigration to the United States.

## The Hart-Celler Act and Recent Latino Migration      1965

On October 3, 1965, President Lyndon Johnson signed the Hart-Celler Act, introducing a new era of mass immigration. The act made people's work skills and their need to unite with their families the most important elements in deciding who could immigrate to the United States. The new legislation eventually ended a system that used people's countries of origin to decide the number of immigrants who were allowed into the United States. The Hart-Celler Act supposedly put people of all nations on an equal footing to immigrate to the United States. The act created the foundation for today's immigration laws.

Between 1960 and 2000, Latin America's population skyrocketed from 218 million to over 520 million. Political instability in the region, in addition to this growing population, meant increased needs for migration and work. Many people turned to the economic opportunities of the United States as a strategy for survival.

At the same time, in the United States, agricultural, industrial, and domestic employers depended upon the ability to pay immigrant laborers from Latin America lower wages. As a result, Latino labor has almost always been welcomed in the United States, despite the government's repeated attempts to restrict immigration in the past century. The demands of U.S. employers for Latino immigrant labor have always shaped the tone of the immigration debate.

## Many Latino Histories

The events of the years 1848, 1898, and 1965 explain how and why Latinos migrated to the United States. However, these events do not

> **Fast Fact**
>
> In 1960, 75 percent of the foreign-born population of the United States came from Europe. Only 14 percent came from Latin America and Asia. As a result of the Hart-Celler Act, by 2000, only 15 percent of immigrants were European and more than 77 percent were Latin American and Asian. This trend promises to continue.

reveal much about what happened once the Latinos arrived. Despite their many shared experiences, Latinos are anything but an easily defined people. Although television and film have tended to portray all Latinos as similar, they come from a wide range of national, ethnic, social, economic, and political backgrounds, which have divided as much as united this growing population. Such backgrounds include "African," "Anglo," "Asian," "Indian," and any combinations of these.

Mexicans started migrating to the United States in the 19th century and Puerto Ricans in the early 20th century. Immigrants from Chile, Argentina, El Salvador, Guatemala, and other South and Central American countries made their way north in large numbers starting in the 1960s. Many of these Latinos were seeking shelter from brutal military dictatorships. Once in the United States, Latinos of all backgrounds have continued to mix with each other and with local populations, forging a whole new set of identities. Latino communities keep and develop their own cultures in new and creative ways in the United States, adding to the rich diversity of the country.

Indeed, Latinos have contributed to U.S. society in other ways besides their investments in the country's economy and labor. In politics, education, sports, and the arts, Latinos are a growing presence. By exploring the origins and development of U.S. Latinos, this series, *Latino American History*, helps us to better understand how our Latin American neighbors to the south have become our Latino neighbors next door.

# Introduction

Latinos have a centuries-old claim to the lands that are now known as the Americas. Some of the first explorers in the New World, as Europeans called these lands, were either Spanish or working for the rulers of Spain: Christopher Columbus, Vasco Núñez de Balboa, Francisco Pizarro, and Hernán Cortés.

These early explorers conquered and enslaved the native people they found already living in the Western Hemisphere. They also had children with native women. These children of mixed Spanish and Indian blood were called mestizos. The descendants of the mestizos would become the people that today are known as the Latinos.

The Spanish explorers left their mark on the present-day United States. One of the first Europeans in North America was Álvar Núñez Cabeza de Vaca, shipwrecked in Texas in 1527. He was followed by Hernando de Soto, who traveled through Florida in 1539, and Francisco Vásquez de Coronado in New Mexico in the early 1540s. These adventurers gave Spain its first claims to what is now the U.S. Southwest.

In the coming decades, Spain would cede most of its claims in North America to England and France. After English colonists won their freedom from England and formed the

OPPOSITE  In August 1999, in New York City's Spanish Harlem, also known as *El Barrio,* muralist James De La Vega poses in front of his mural, which reflects the spirit of the neighborhood where it stands.

United States, Spain had yet another powerful nation to contend with for its land in the Western Hemisphere.

## Latinos and the United States

In 1821, Spain's largest and most important colony, Mexico, won its independence. At this time, Mexico included all or parts of present-day Texas, California, New Mexico, Arizona, Nevada, Utah, Colorado, and Wyoming. These regions were soon targeted by U.S. settlers from the East. After the Mexican-American War (1846–1848), a defeated Mexico was forced to forfeit all its land north of the Rio Grande to its neighbor, the United States. The people who had once thought of themselves as Spanish or Mexican were now U.S. citizens—the first Latino Americans in the nation.

In the coming years, many more Latinos would migrate to the United States from Mexico and the Caribbean, as well as from Central and South America. Many came to the country to avoid political turmoil at home as their nations declared freedom from Spanish rule. Others came to find jobs and make better lives for themselves and their families.

Latinos, like other immigrant groups, have helped make the United States a great nation. They worked on railroads and in factories, constructed the nation's roads and buildings, and harvested the food that U.S. residents ate. They also brought their unique cultures to the places they settled. Today, this cultural influence can be experienced in the Southwest and in Latino-dominated neighborhoods like Spanish Harlem in New York and Little Havana in Florida.

In the early 20th century, Latino Americans sacrificed their lives for the United States, fighting bravely in World War I (1914–1918). Many Latinos fought side by side with Anglos for the cause of freedom. Despite their willingness to die for their country, however, Latinos and other minority groups were not treated fairly by many Anglo Americans at the beginning of the 20th century. In the workplace, they were given menial, low-paying jobs with few benefits. In many communities, they were forced to live in the poorest, most crowded neighborhoods. In some public places, signs warned that Latinos were not allowed to eat, swim, or play with Anglos. Their children were even forced to go to segregated, or separate, schools.

In the 1930s, during the Great Depression, discrimination and anti-Latino sentiment skyrocketed in the United States. Mexican Americans were rounded up by the thousands and repatriated, or sent back to Mexico. This unfair treatment spurred Latinos to band together, forming groups and unions to protect their rights. In time, these groups would empower Latinos and enable them to fight for their rights as U.S. citizens.

# Latinos and World War II

1

The early 1940s were difficult times for many U.S. citizens, including Latinos. Most people in the United States were still recovering from the Great Depression, the period in the 1930s marked by a poor economy and mass unemployment.

During the Great Depression, some people resented Mexicans and other Latino immigrants. They thought the new arrivals were taking jobs away from Anglo Americans. The U.S. government hoped that repatriation would open more jobs for Anglo Americans. People who were repatriated were forced to return to their native countries. As the largest Latino group in the United States, Mexicans were the key target of repatriation efforts. About 500,000 Mexicans who could not prove they had entered the country legally were forced to leave. Many Latinos who remained in the United States—including legal immigrants and U.S. citizens—lost their jobs or failed to find new ones as companies went out of business or hired out-of-work Anglos to fill empty positions. In 1933, President Franklin

OPPOSITE  About 500,000 Latinos served for the United States in World War II, including about 65,000 Puerto Ricans, such as the men shown here.

Roosevelt started the New Deal, a series of social programs intended to help U.S. citizens suffering during the Great Depression. Many Latinos received jobs or aid. Still, Mexicans received less money than Anglo Americans.

Latinos who managed to keep their jobs also faced problems. Many were expected to work longer hours for less pay. Farm workers faced very harsh treatment. Some formed unions. A union is an organization of workers set up to improve such things as working conditions, wages, and health benefits. Growers often opposed unions because they drove up the cost of labor by demanding better wages and other benefits for workers.

Struggles between workers and growers sometimes erupted into strikes and violence. In 1933, for example, 1,800 cotton pickers in California's Central Valley walked off the fields to protest a cut in wages. Three out of four of these striking cotton pickers were Mexican. In response, farm owners threw the workers out of company-owned living quarters, known as workers' camps. Then the growers called in police and armed Anglo citizens to intimidate the striking workers. Strike leaders were arrested, and two strikers were killed in the struggle.

The Great Depression was one of the darkest periods in U.S. history. However, conditions were about to change. On December 7, 1941, Japan attacked Pearl Harbor, Hawaii, and the United States entered World War II (1939–1945). During this war, the United States, France, Great Britain, the Soviet Union, and other allied nations defeated Germany, Italy, and Japan. World War II had far-reaching effects on the lives of many Latinos in the United States.

## Latinos Who Fought in World War II

During World War II, the armed forces offered a chance for Latinos to show their patriotism and loyalty to the United States. The military also offered a way out of poverty for many Latinos. As a result, a greater percentage of Latinos volunteered for the armed forces during World War II than any other group of U.S. citizens. About 500,000 Latinos served in the U.S. armed forces, including 400,000 Mexican Americans and 65,000 Puerto Ricans.

Because of the large number of Latinos from southwestern states like Texas and New Mexico, many units from these areas consisted mainly of Mexican Americans. The Santa Fe Battalion from New Mexico was one of these units. The battalion served in Africa, building a railroad across the North African desert. The Allies used the railroad to ship supplies to soldiers fighting German and Italian troops.

On December 10, 1941, just three days after Pearl Harbor was bombed, Japan invaded the Philippines, a U.S. possession. The U.S. Army

### Rewarded for Bravery

The U.S. military awards special medals for servicemen and servicewomen who perform acts of valor, or bravery. Many Latino soldiers earned medals during World War II. The highest military decoration is the Congressional Medal of Honor. Joseph P. Martinez was one Mexican American who won a Medal of Honor. Martinez was a 22-year-old farm worker in Colorado when he was drafted into the U.S. Army. Private Martinez came under Japanese attack in the Aleutian Islands. He charged forward into a Japanese-held position while under heavy fire. Unfortunately, he died from injuries he received during his assault. After his death, Martinez became the first Latino in World War II to be awarded the Medal of Honor. A statue of him can be seen in Denver, Colorado.

## Fighting for American Values

Latinos who were awarded the Medal of Honor during World War II had enlisted in military units that were based in the states highlighted in green on the map.

stationed many Latino soldiers in the Philippines. The Philippines had been a Spanish colony from 1565 to 1898, and many people there, including soldiers, still spoke Spanish. Most Latinos also spoke Spanish, as well as English. This ability helped them work well with the Filipino soldiers.

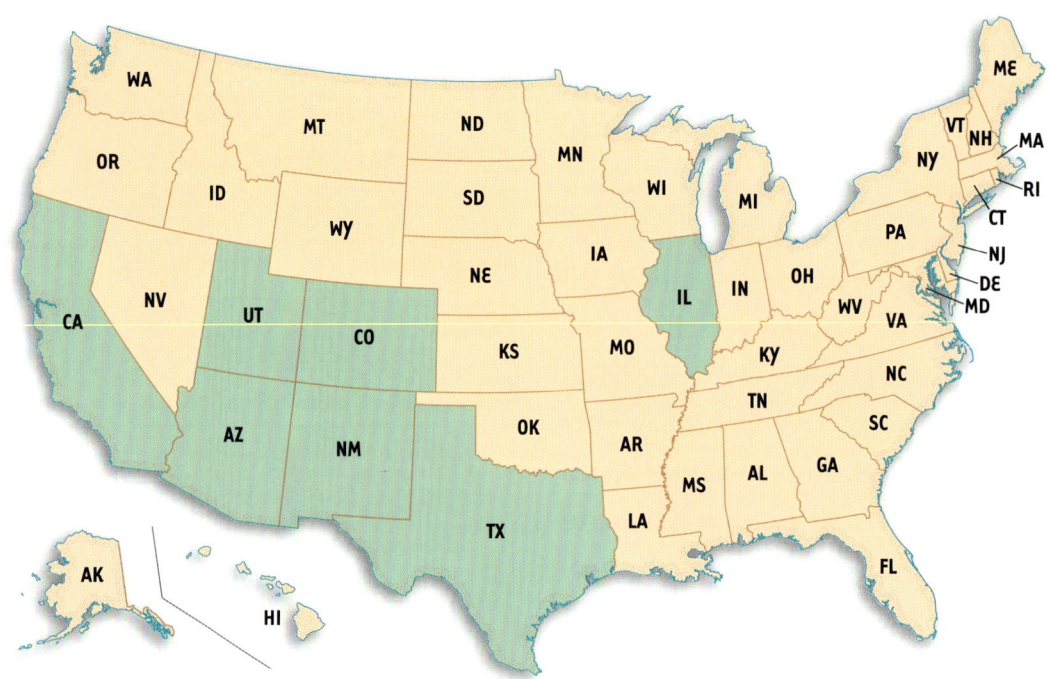

## Latinos on the Home Front

When the United States joined the war, many factories began manufacturing weapons and other goods needed for the war effort. The economy recovered, and the pain of the Great Depression slowly faded from memory. However, most of the traditional U.S. workforce was away fighting the war. The need for workers created new opportunities for many people in the United States, including Latinos. Many Latinos—both men and women—left farms and small towns and moved to large cities to work in war factories.

For Latinos, the labor shortage offered a chance to find new kinds of employment. Until then, many Latinos had been discriminated against during the hiring process. It was hard for them to find skilled or even semi-skilled jobs, so before World War II, they mostly worked on farms and in service jobs. The war changed this pattern. President Roosevelt created the Fair Employment Practices Committee (FEPC) in 1941. The committee required that any company making or supplying goods for the federal government had to treat people equally, regardless of ethnic background.

The FEPC helped Latinos and other ethnic minorities find better jobs and receive deserved promotions. In his role as special assistant to the FEPC, Carlos Castañeda improved employment conditions for Mexican Americans in Texas. Castañeda was a Mexican immigrant who had moved to Texas with his family when he was 10 years old. He

## Castañeda's Words

Carlos Castañeda asked politicians to improve conditions for Latinos in the workforce. Below is part of a speech he gave to a Senate committee in 1941.

*The prevalent . . . belief among employers for the various industries . . . and government agencies in the Southwest is that the Mexican-American is . . . unfit for the . . . skilled labor required by industry and the crafts. . . . Equal economic opportunities, the right to work and earn a decent living on a par with all other persons regardless of race, creed, color, national origin or ancestry, is a basic principle of American democracy.*

became a historian and taught at the University of Texas. Among his accomplishments was an FEPC order he wrote demanding that a Texas oil company treat Latinos equally. As a result, the percentage of Latinos in skilled and semi-skilled jobs at the company rose from 15 percent in 1930 to about 35 percent in 1950.

During World War II, army transports carried many workers from Puerto Rico to the United States to fill jobs in the war industry. At the start of the war, more than 61,000 Puerto Ricans made their homes in New York. By 1950, that figure nearly quadrupled, to about 246,000 Puerto Ricans in New York.

## The Bracero Program

Even with many women and minority people entering the workforce, U.S. businesses were still in desperate need of help. After deporting Mexicans with the repatriation program, the United States now turned to them for aid. The U.S. and Mexican governments created the bracero program in July 1942 as a way to end the labor shortage.

Braceros were hired Mexican laborers who were transported from Mexico into the United States. They were guaranteed equal treatment and a minimum wage of 30 cents an hour. This wage was less than business owners would have to pay U.S. workers, but far more than the average salary in Mexico. As a result, more than 250,000 Mexicans worked in

> **Fast Fact**
> 
> The word *bracero* comes from *brazo,* the Spanish word for "arm." A bracero is "someone who works with his arms."

the bracero program between 1942 and 1947. Most braceros worked on farms and railroads. When the work season was finished, braceros returned to Mexico with the money they had saved.

As part of the bracero program, the Mexican government required that the braceros be protected against discrimination. However, there was still much unfair treatment, especially in Texas. For example, in 1944, a café in Laredo, Texas, posted a racist sign saying, "Negroes, Mexicans, and dogs not allowed." Because of such harsh discrimination, the Mexican government refused to allow any more braceros to work in Texas.

A Mexican worker arrives in California by train in 1942 during the early days of the bracero program. Thousands of Mexican workers came to the United States during World War II to work on farms and railroads.

## Latinos Face Challenges

Many people respected Latinos for their help with the U.S. war effort. Latinos took new jobs in industry. Many Latino servicemen returning from the war used the resources of the G.I. Bill to go to school. (Congress passed the G.I. Bill of Rights in 1944 to provide returning World War II veterans, known as G.I.s, with funding for education, loans for buying homes, and other benefits.) Despite these positive changes, however, Latinos still faced prejudice back home.

The Sleepy Lagoon Case showed how deep was the prejudice against Mexican Americans. On August 2, 1942, José Díaz was found beaten to death near the Sleepy Lagoon Reservoir, a holding area for water near Los Angeles, California. In response, police arrested more than 600 Mexican Americans, claiming they had something to do with the case. In one of the largest mass trials in history, 24 of the arrested Mexican Americans were charged with murder. The lawyers and the judge were openly prejudiced against the defendants. One "expert" witness claimed that "this Mexican element feels a desire to kill or at least draw blood." Although no witnesses saw Díaz being stabbed, 17 of the youths were convicted of crimes. Two years later, an appeals court overturned the verdict because of the judge's extreme prejudice. The case was not reopened, and the murder of the young man remains unsolved.

One of the worst attacks on Latinos happened in 1943 in Los Angeles. At that time, the city had a large Mexican-American population. Many of the Mexican-American teenagers wore a popular, flashy style of clothing known as the zoot suit. The outfit consisted of a long, oversized jacket with large padded shoulders and baggy pants with snug cuffs at the ankles. Young Mexican-American men who wore zoot suits were called pachucos.

The two youths in the center, one stripped of all his clothes and the other badly beaten, fell victim to raging bands of white servicemen in Los Angeles who beat up Latinos that they blamed for numerous assaults on their colleagues in June 1943.

The zoot suit riots began on June 3, 1943. A group of 11 sailors told police that they had been walking though a Mexican neighborhood when pachucos attacked them. The truth was that the sailors had started the fight. For two weeks afterward, the streets of Los Angeles were a battlefield between Anglo servicemen and Mexican Americans. Large groups of sailors, soldiers, and civilians roamed the streets, attacking Mexican Americans. Police usually sided with the Anglo servicemen. One eyewitness described an attack:

*Four boys came out of a pool hall. They were wearing the zoot-suits that have become the symbol of a fighting flag. Police ordered them into arrest cars. One refused. He asked: "Why am I being arrested?" The police officer answered with three swift blows of the night-stick across the boy's head and he went down. As he sprawled, he was kicked in the face. Police had difficulty loading his body into the vehicle because he was one-legged and wore a wooden limb.*

Finally, the U.S. government ordered military police to take action. The military police started arresting sailors and soldiers, and the zoot suit riots ended. Still, the riots spread prejudice against Mexican Americans to other areas of the United States. There were attacks on Mexican Americans in Texas, Illinois, Indiana, Pennsylvania, and New York.

To help end discrimination, the Texas government passed the Caucasian Race Resolution in 1944. This law declared that all people of Mexican descent were white and should receive equal treatment. (At this time, black people were treated as second-class citizens throughout most of the United States.) Even with this law, many public places in Texas continued to be segregated, meaning Mexicans were kept apart from Anglos.

Even war heroes were not safe from discrimination. Félix Longoria was a U.S. soldier who died fighting on a volunteer mission in the Philippines during the war. His body was recovered in 1948 and brought back to the United States for burial. Officials at the only funeral home in Longoria's hometown of Three Rivers, Texas, refused to allow his family to hold a wake there because he was Mexican-American. The funeral director explained his refusal by saying that "the whites would not like it."

Longoria's unfair treatment made the national news, and many people became very upset about this discrimination against a war hero. The American G.I. Forum became involved in the issue. Dr. Héctor García had founded this civil rights organization in 1948 to use political pressure to fight racial discrimination against Mexican Americans. García wrote letters to Texas politicians, complaining of the discrimination. In response, Senator Lyndon B. Johnson arranged for Longoria to be buried with full honors at Arlington National Cemetery on February 16, 1949.

# Latinos in Postwar Society

## 2

After World War II, the U.S. government worked to prevent another global threat: the spread of communism. Although the United States had been allied with the communist Soviet Union during World War II, the relationship between the two superpowers quickly fell apart once the war was over. The Soviet Union installed communist governments in Eastern European countries it had "liberated" from German control during the war. Then the Soviets began looking toward Asia to expand their influence.

The United States wanted to stop the spread of communism. U.S. officials particularly wanted to keep this political ideology out of the Western Hemisphere. In order to do this, the United States felt justified in stepping in and interfering with Latin American affairs if socialist or communist groups looked like they might take power in a nation. Beginning in the early 1960s, the United States would become involved in the affairs of Guatemala, Cuba, the Dominican Republic, and other nations in order to stop communism from taking root there.

OPPOSITE Communist Cuban leaders march together in March 1960. They include Fidel Castro (left) and Ernesto "Che" Guevara (center).

## Working in the United States

The bracero program continued for two years after the end of World War II. When the program came to an end in 1947, about 200,000 braceros were working in 21 states, mostly in Texas and California. Many of these laborers were working in the fields, harvesting sugar beets, cotton, lettuce, tomatoes, and other crops throughout the Southwest. Other braceros drove trucks or worked on U.S. railroads.

> **Fast Fact**
>
> The period of tension and rivalry between countries that supported communism and those that supported democracy became known as the Cold War (1945–1991). The Soviet Union and the United States were the two chief rivals during this period, which lasted for more than four decades.

Farmers and other business owners were not happy when the program ended. The low wages they had paid the braceros meant reduced costs and increased profits. So U.S. business interests lobbied Congress for the braceros to return, and the program was quickly restarted in 1948.

## Protecting Workers' Rights

After World War II, the braceros continued to be treated poorly. They were paid less than other workers and forced to live in squalid conditions. In a 1960 television documentary called *Harvest of Shame,* a farmer talked about his migrant workers: "We used to own our slaves. Now we just rent them."

In 1948, Texas cotton growers lowered the maximum wage payable to braceros. The Mexican workers would now receive 50 cents an hour less than all other workers.

Mexican officials were furious and forbade their laborers to work the Texas cotton harvest until growers agreed to pay them equal wages. The Mexican military lined the border between the two countries to prevent workers from entering the United States.

The Immigration and Naturalization Service (INS) stepped in to help the Texas cotton growers. INS officials opened up the border, allowing Mexicans looking for jobs to pour in. Growers waiting at the borders piled the braceros into trucks and transported them to labor camps to work. The U.S. government apologized for the incident, but only after the harvest was over.

In the 1950s, these braceros were photographed heading for El Paso, Texas, from Chihuahua, Mexico.

One man who was concerned with the treatment of migrant workers was César Chávez. In 1952, he founded Mexican-American branches of the Community Service Organization (CSO) in California and Arizona. Through the CSO, Chávez and other labor organizers, such as Dolores Huerta, registered migrant workers to vote and helped them fight for other rights.

The bracero program was permanently ended in 1964. During the nearly two decades the program was in effect, about 4.5 million Mexicans took part. The late 1950s were the

## César Chávez

César Estrada Chávez (1927–1993) was born in Yuma, Arizona. His father and mother were migrant workers who had moved to the United States. Chávez served in the U.S. Navy during World War II. After the war, he returned to picking crops. Later, he and his wife, Helen, moved to San Jose, California, where he worked at the Community Service Organization (CSO), a group that helped communities win important rights. In 1962, Chávez moved to Delano, California, where he organized migrant farm workers into the National Farm Workers Association (later known as the United Farm Workers). In 1966, his group merged with the American Federation of Labor and Congress of Industrial Organizations (AFL-CIO), one of the largest and most powerful unions in the United States.

In the coming years, Chávez would help organize hunger strikes, rallies, and other nonviolent means of resistance. His efforts shone a light on the plight of the migrant worker. Chávez died in 1993.

key years for the program. After the program ended, Mexican laborers were still given entry to the United States via "green cards," special permits that allowed the workers to stay in the country for the purpose of temporary employment.

> **Fast Fact**
>
> During the 1950s, about 273,800 Mexicans immigrated legally to the United States with the proper documentation.

## Entering Illegally

During the 1950s, Mexicans without the necessary documents avoided INS officials at the border by wading across the Rio Grande. Those who made the dangerous trip in search of higher-paying jobs and a higher standard of living were labeled wetbacks *(mojados)* by some Anglos, an insulting term that described how they sneaked across the big river. Because of the high numbers of undocumented immigrants entering the United States from Mexico, the 10 years from 1944 to 1954 became known as the "decade of the wetback." Illegal immigration from Mexico to the United States increased by about 6,000 percent during this time.

Once over the border, undocumented immigrants found plenty of employers who were willing to hire them. These new, undocumented arrivals were given agricultural, industrial, and service jobs in the Southwest, Midwest, and West. The jobs almost always paid low wages and offered few benefits—jobs that legal immigrants and U.S. citizens scorned. Although it was against the law for employers to hire undocumented workers, many took the chance. It allowed them to dodge minimum wage requirements and other labor laws.

Once undocumented immigrants accepted a job, they were at the mercy of their employers. These employers could report them to immigration authorities at will. Unscrupulous employers sometimes fired their workers before paying them or reported them to the INS once the job was finished. The workers had no protections from such abuse.

Undocumented immigrants were also the targets of government deportation programs. In 1950, the U.S. government started a massive repatriation program to round up and deport Mexicans working illegally in the United States. Between 1950 and 1955, government agents raided workplaces and homes, searching for undocumented Mexicans. They stopped Latinos on the streets, asking them to show their immigration documents. During the five-year period the program was in effect, 3.8 million Mexicans were sent back to Mexico. Some of those who were sent back had already lived in the United States for many years.

## Latinos and the Korean War

In 1950, the United States became involved in a war between communist North Korea and democratic South Korea. During the Korean War (1950–1953), the United States, along with many other democratic countries and the United Nations, supported South Korea; the Soviet Union and communist China supported North Korea.

In the hopes of preventing communism from spreading into South Korea, the United States sent more than 5 million troops to fight there. About 148,000 of these men and women were Latinos. The service helped Latinos assimilate, or fit in, to U.S. culture. In the military, Latinos not only were trained to fight, but also learned to speak English.

One group of Latinos was the 65th Infantry, a regiment made up of more than 43,000 Puerto Rican soldiers. The men in this regiment fought in nine major operations during the war. After the war, the entire regiment received two Presidential Unit Citations, a Meritorious Unit Commendation, and many other honors. Their commander, General William W. Harris, wrote: "No ethnic group has greater pride in itself and its heritage than the Puerto Rican people. Nor have I encountered any that can be more dedicated and zealous in support of the democratic principles for which the United States stands. Many Puerto Ricans have fought to the death to uphold them."

Francisco Leon Rosa (bottom, second from the right), shown here with his unit in Hausberg, Germany, in 1954, was one of the thousands of Latinos who served in the U.S. Army in the 1950s.

## The Maquiladora Program

In 1965, Mexico started a maquiladora program along the U.S.-Mexican border. The new program allowed U.S. companies to build factories in Mexico along the border. The factories employed cheap Mexican labor to assemble U.S. products. These products were then shipped, tax-free, back into the United States. The term *maquiladora* came to mean a factory that assembled duty-free imported goods for export. The goal of the new program was to employ Mexican workers who had lost their jobs when the bracero program came to an end in 1964.

The program resulted in the rapid growth of many Mexican border towns, including Matamoros, Mexicali, and Tijuana. The people who received the most benefit, however, were the U.S. business owners. Once again, they were able to evade U.S. labor laws and take advantage of cheap Mexican labor.

---

By the end of the war, nine Latinos had received the Congressional Medal of Honor for their bravery. Hundreds more received other honors for their wartime service. Once the Korean War was over, however, Latino veterans who had fought side by side with white soldiers came home to find themselves the victims of racial discrimination in housing and employment and throughout society.

## U.S. Immigration Policy— Federal and Local

In the 1960s, legal immigration from Mexico continued to increase dramatically. Like those before them, the new arrivals from Mexico left their homes to escape unemployment and poverty. During this decade, people from Mexico made up 13.3 percent of all immigrants to the United States.

Illegal immigration also increased. These undocumented workers continued to be exploited by employers. They were also targeted for harassment and violence by labor leaders, Anglo workers, and others.

In 1965, legal immigration became even more difficult for people from Mexico. That year, Congress passed the Immigration and Nationality Act. The new law, which took effect in 1968, limited the number of immigrants from anywhere in the Western Hemisphere to just 120,000 people. In 1978, Congress capped immigration from any single country at 20,000 people. Despite these new quotas, four out of ten immigrants to the United States still came from Latin America and the Caribbean.

In the decade after the new laws were passed, as many as 5 million Mexicans entered the country illegally. In response, the U.S. government established even more programs to identify and deport undocumented immigrants.

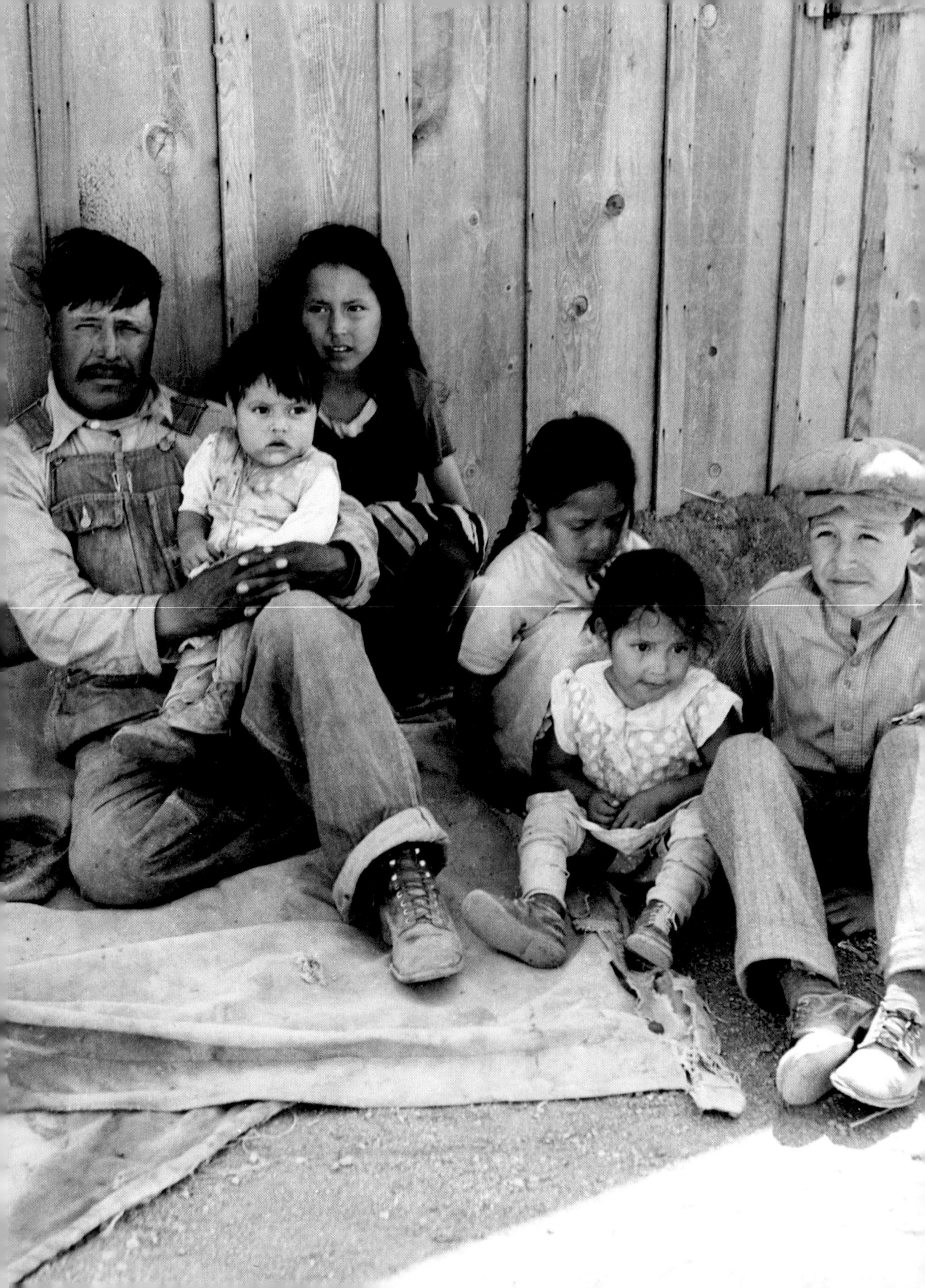

# New Latino Arrivals from the Americas

## 3

Many of the Mexicans who settled in the United States after World War II followed earlier Mexicans to barrios, or neighborhoods, in big cities around the nation. At the beginning of the 1950s, 66 percent of all Mexican Americans lived in cities. This percentage would increase rapidly in the coming years. By 1970, 85 percent would live in urban areas.

The majority of Mexicans continued to make their homes in the Southwest. They chose this region because of its closeness to Mexico and because Latino barrios were already well established there. In the Mexican neighborhoods, new arrivals could hear Spanish spoken everywhere. They could shop at stores that specialized in Mexican goods, eat in restaurants that cooked Mexican food, and read Spanish-language newspapers. In turn, these immigrants rejuvenated and reinforced Mexican culture in the United States.

After World War II, many Mexicans moved to other parts of the United States, particularly the Midwest. These Latinos were looking for better jobs and living conditions. They

OPPOSITE After World War II, Mexican families in the United States faced different challenges than those before the war—such as this Mexican migrant family shown in Colorado in 1936—had faced.

found employment in factories, steel mills, meat-processing plants, and other industries. They, too, chose to live in Latino neighborhoods, established by the generation of Mexican workers before them.

## Life for Mexican Americans after World War II

In some ways, Mexican immigrants after World War II were very different from previous generations of Mexican Americans. For example, the Spanish that they spoke was different from the Spanish that was spoken throughout the Southwest. Earlier arrivals now spoke a dialect that included a combination of both Spanish and English. Earlier arrivals had also adapted to life in the United States to varying degrees. Many wanted the latest Mexican immigrants to assimilate quickly. They believed that the key to success in the United States was to adopt Anglo customs. They wanted to be sure that the new arrivals did not have a negative impact on the way U.S. citizens viewed Mexican Americans.

The new arrivals also had things in common with earlier immigrants. For example, the large, extended family—parents, children, grandparents, aunts, uncles, cousins, and godparents, or compadres—remained the focus of Mexican-American communities. In addition, Mexicans, whether recently arrived or long established in the United States, enjoyed celebrating Mexican holidays, especially Mexican Independence Day (September 16) and Cinco de Mayo (May 5). These cultural occasions allowed the entire Mexican American community to celebrate its common heritage.

However, all Mexicans continued to be the target of prejudice and unfair treatment, especially in the Southwest. Latinos there suffered from the same types of open discrimination that African Americans in the Southeast did. Latinos were not permitted to eat in Anglo restaurants, swim in Anglo pools, or drink from Anglo water fountains. Some communities even prohibited Mexicans from living in their neighborhoods. In some towns and cities, Mexican children and Anglo children were educated in separate schools. The Mexican schools were inferior to the ones Anglos attended,

*Mexican braceros pick chili peppers in California in 1964.*

and the Latino children were usually forced to speak English only, with no help in Spanish. In some places, the children of migrant workers were not allowed to attend school at all.

Such unfair treatment was not new. It had been going on for decades. Some Mexicans felt that the way to overcome such treatment was to learn English and fit in with Anglo culture. During the 1950s, for example, the League of United Latin American Citizens (LULAC) established preschools to teach Mexican-American children 400 English words. But in the coming decades, many Mexicans would reject the idea that they should have to assimilate in order to be accepted. Instead, they would choose to fight for their civil rights as human beings and U.S. citizens.

## Central American Immigrants

Mexicans were not the only Latinos migrating to the United States after World War II. During the 1950s and 1960s, immigration from many Central American countries also increased. At this time, many Latin American nations were plagued by economic instability, rapid population growth, and violent political unrest. The unrest in Latin America would continue throughout the 1970s and into the 1980s. U.S. officials contributed to the problems in Latin America by sending money and guns to government or rebel groups that the United States wanted in power.

The number of Central American immigrants to the United States jumped as more and more people fled the violence and instability of their home countries. By 1970, about 174,000 Central Americans had migrated to the

United States. The influx of immigrants from this region would truly skyrocket after 1980, when tens of thousands of people fled the war-torn nations of El Salvador, Guatemala, and Nicaragua.

Unlike other Latino immigrant groups, many of the Central American immigrants during the 1970s were women. Up to 28 percent of all immigrants from the region were domestic workers, such as maids or housekeepers. Other immigrants from Central America at this time were professionals and white-collar workers hoping to earn more money in the United States.

> **Fast Fact**
>
> In 1979, President Jimmy Carter negotiated a treaty with Panama that gave control of the Panama Canal back to Panama. The handover became official in 2000.

Like many other Latino immigrants, those from Central America chose to settle in urban areas. Most of the new arrivals moved to western or southern cities like Los Angeles and San Francisco, California, or Miami, Florida. However, many people from Panama and Honduras settled in New York City instead.

## South American Immigrants

During the decades after World War II, South America suffered many of the same problems as some of its Central American neighbors. As in Central America, the United States interfered, hoping to influence the outcome of civil wars and political uprisings.

One country that was especially violent was Colombia. From 1948 to 1962, the nation suffered from civil unrest that the people nicknamed *La Violencia.* During this time, thousands of people fled the country to escape the violence. They also left to escape a weak economy and high unemployment. Other nations that suffered from political turmoil were Uruguay, Chile, and Argentina.

Immigration from Central and South America continued throughout the 1970s. From 1967 to 1976, the countries in Central America with the highest number of immigrants to the United States were Guatemala, El Salvador, and Panama, and the highest number of South American immigrants came from Colombia, Ecuador, and Argentina.

Most immigrants from South America chose the Northeast as their primary destination. For Colombians, New York City was a favorite spot, with many choosing the borough of Queens as their new home. Groups of immigrants from the Dominican Republic, Argentina, and Ecuador also settled in Queens.

Like other Latino groups who created strong ethnic enclaves in the United States, Central and South Americans tried to re-create the life they had known in their former homes. For example, immigrants opened bodegas (grocery stores), restaurants, and other businesses to cater to their needs, and Latin American customs were retained.

## Latino Culture and the Pressure to Assimilate

In the early days of Latino immigration, Spanish-speaking immigrants from Mexico and other Latin American countries were expected to adopt English as their primary language and to embrace the culture and practices of their new home. Such expectations continued after World War II. New Latino immigrants who refused to assimilate or had difficulty adapting were unfavorably compared with previous waves of U.S. immigrants, such as the Irish or Italians.

One way that the United States imposed its culture upon Latinos was through the educational system. In schools, Latino children were expected to speak English. Bilingual education, or the teaching of Latino children in Spanish and English, did not become common until the 1970s.

In the 1950s, television became another important means of promoting assimilation. Watching television promoted the English language and U.S. cultural values.

The new medium, however, also boosted racist stereotypes about Latinos. One of the first Latino television stereotypes was the character of Ricky Ricardo. Ricardo was a hotheaded, barely understandable Latino bandleader played by Cuban immigrant Desi Arnaz. Arnaz, acting

## A Movie for Latino Workers

In 1954, a film called *Salt of the Earth* told the story of a strike by Mexican workers at a New Mexico zinc mine in 1950. The film was unusual in that it presented a sympathetic portrayal of Latino workers and featured Latinos in the lead roles.

The film's pro-union message quickly stirred up controversy. During the filming of the movie, the lead actress, Mexican Rosaura Revueltas, was arrested by the INS and deported. The movie was labeled communist propaganda, and the filmmakers were shot at when they filmed on location in New Mexico. Back in Hollywood, studios refused to allow the filmmakers to use their facilities for editing and other postproduction jobs. Because of studio and political pressure, *Salt of the Earth* was shown in only a handful of theaters. Today, the film has received new attention and is well regarded.

opposite his wife Lucille Ball in the comedy series *I Love Lucy,* played the straight man to Ball's wacky redhead.

In the 1950s, Latino businessmen began producing programs in Spanish for Anglo television. As in the early days of radio, the Latino entrepreneurs purchased time slots on Anglo TV stations in order to air their programs. In 1955, the first Spanish-language television station, KCOR-TV, went on the air in San Antonio. The station had viewing hours from five o'clock in the evening until midnight. It featured variety shows, live entertainment, movies, and other prerecorded programs from Mexico. In the coming years, the Latino presence on television would increase.

Lucille Ball and Desi Arnaz were well regarded as the stars of TV's *I Love Lucy* in the 1950s. However, Arnaz's character, Cuban immigrant Ricky Ricardo, helped reinforce Latino stereotypes.

During the 1950s, the first U.S. Spanish-language magazine was published. The magazine, called *Temas (Themes)*, saw its first printing in November 1950 in New York City. Aimed at Latino families, it featured interviews with famous people, articles on culture, current events, and fashion, and much more. The magazine was the first of several that would crop up in the coming years as Latino Americans embraced ways to hold on to their language and culture.

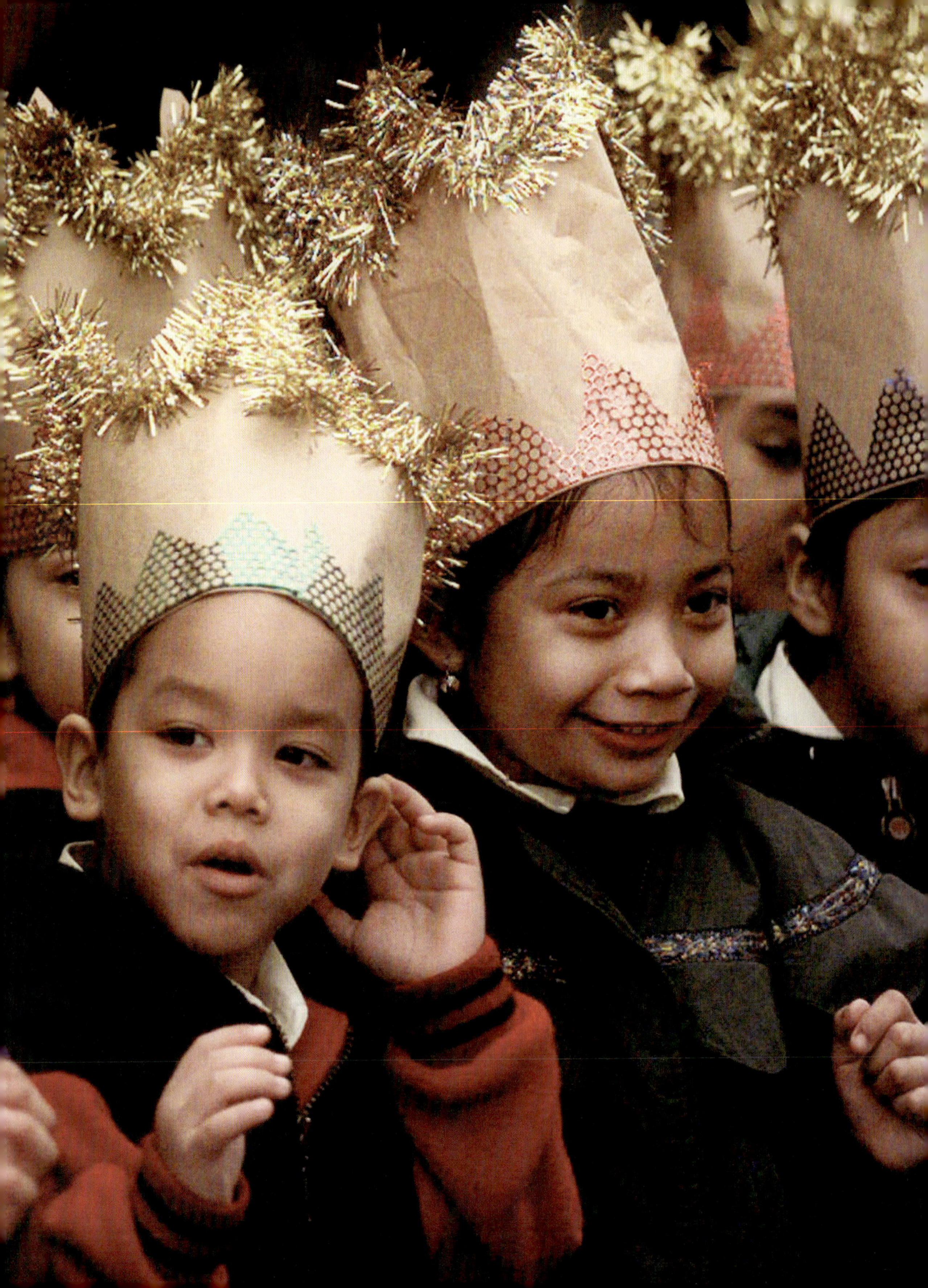

# The Great Migration from Puerto Rico

4

The movement of people between Puerto Rico and the U.S. mainland is known as migration, not immigration. This is because Puerto Ricans have been U.S. citizens since 1917. U.S. involvement in the small island's affairs began after the United States defeated Spain in the Spanish-American War (1898). After the war, Puerto Rico became a U.S. protectorate. A protectorate is a nation that is protected by a larger, more powerful one.

In 1900, Congress passed the Foraker Act. This act placed U.S. citizens in charge of Puerto Rico's government. The new law also set up a 35-member House of Representatives elected by the people of Puerto Rico, as well as a Supreme Court and judicial system. Additionally, the act gave islanders a voice in the U.S. Congress by creating the role of a nonvoting resident commissioner. However, the people of Puerto Rico were not considered U.S. citizens. Although they were subject to the same national laws, they did not have the same rights that citizens on the mainland enjoyed.

OPPOSITE Students in Spanish Harlem celebrate Three Kings Day in December 1998. This Latino custom honors the three kings who visited the Christ child at his birth.

In March 1917, just one month before the United States entered World War I, President Woodrow Wilson signed a law that gave U.S. citizenship to Puerto Ricans. As U.S. citizens, Puerto Ricans could now come and go between the mainland and their island without any restrictions. Yet they were still not given the full rights and obligations of U.S. citizens on the mainland. For example, they were exempt from federal income taxes and could not vote in national elections. They could, however, be drafted into the U.S. military. Thousands of Puerto Ricans served bravely during World War I and World War II. Many remained on the mainland once these wars ended.

## Puerto Rican Politics in the Mid-1900s

President Roosevelt worked to reverse some discriminatory policies against Puerto Rico, and he set up government agencies to improve conditions on the island. However, many Puerto Ricans wanted nothing less than independence for their island, and the 1930s saw many independence movements start. In 1936 and 1937, Congress failed to pass bills to make Puerto Rico self-governing.

After Roosevelt's death, Puerto Ricans continued to make strides toward greater self-rule. In 1946, U.S. officials appointed Jésus T. Piñero as the first native governor of Puerto Rico. The following year, Congress passed an act allowing the citizens of Puerto Rico to elect their own governor. In 1948, Luis Muñoz Marín became the first native governor chosen by Puerto Ricans themselves.

In 1952, Puerto Ricans went to the polls and approved a new constitution for the island. Under the terms of the constitution, Puerto Rico became a "free associated state," or, in English terms, a commonwealth. A commonwealth is a nation that depends upon another country for some things, such as funds or military defense, but still has the power to make its own laws and elect its own government.

## The Independentistas

A small group of Puerto Ricans refused to accept anything less than independence for their island. These *independentistas*, as they were known, sometimes resorted to violence to bring attention to their cause. In 1950, two Puerto Rican men, Oscar Collazo and Griselio Torresola, failed in an attempt to assassinate President Harry S. Truman. One of Truman's bodyguards was killed in the assault, as was Torresola. Collazo was later sentenced to death, but President Truman changed the sentence to life in prison.

### Operation Bootstrap

In 1948, *Operación Manos a la Obra* (Operation Hands to Work) got its start. The goal of the project, known more commonly as Operation Bootstrap, was to industrialize Puerto Rico. Factories were built across the island to take advantage of the large pool of cheap labor. Many of the factories were owned by U.S. businesses on the mainland.

Operation Bootstrap had its successes and its failures. At first, the project strengthened Puerto Rico by transforming the economy from agriculture to industry. Improved sanitation, roads, and education benefited the people on the island. But because the new industries did not provide enough work for Puerto Rican laborers, many people were left unemployed. Operation Bootstrap, meant to be an economic boon to the island, ended up being one of the major causes of the Great Migration to the mainland.

## Fighting for American Values

From left to right are Rafael Cancel Miranda, Andrés Figueroa Cordero, Lolita Lebrón, and Irving Flores at the federal courthouse in Washington, D.C., during their arraignment for wounding five members of Congress in a 1954 shooting.

Less than four years later, four Puerto Rican independentistas made headlines when they attacked the U.S. House of Representatives in Washington, D.C. Andrés Figueroa Cordero, Irving Flores, and Rafael Cancel Miranda, led by Lolita Lebrón, opened fire from the visitors' gallery as the politicians below them debated an immigration bill. In all, 30 shots were fired and five congressmen were wounded. All four of the shooters were captured and given long prison sentences. Cordero was released in 1977, and the rest were set free two years later. Today, Lebrón continues to work for Puerto Rican independence.

## The Great Migration Begins

After World War II, Puerto Rican migration to the mainland soared. With the advent of cheap—and quick—air travel between Puerto Rico and New York, about 20,000 Puerto Ricans chose to move to the mainland each year in search of better jobs and opportunities. The boom in migration also spurred a boom in the airline business. By 1947, more than 20 airlines offered flights to and from Puerto Rico.

The movement of people to the mainland from Puerto Rico from the mid-1940s through the 1970s became known as the Great Migration. During this time, more than 1.4 million people left the island. More than half of these migrants chose to settle in New York. Between 1940 and 1970, the number of Puerto Ricans living in New York jumped from 61,463 to 860,552. During some parts of the 1970s, however, as jobs in the region became scarce, more people returned to the island than came to the mainland.

Many Puerto Ricans who came to the United States during the Great Migration were contract laborers—uneducated young men with few job skills who were hired to work in fields and factories on the mainland. Most of these migrants intended to return to the island after earning some money. However, many remained on the mainland, sending for friends and family members once they were settled in their new homes.

> **Fast Fact**
>
> Puerto Ricans who live in or were born in New York are sometimes called *Nuyoricans*. After the Great Migration, the word Nuyorican was also used to describe the literature, music, and other arts that Puerto Ricans in New York had developed.

## Making a New Home in Spanish Harlem

Many of the postwar arrivals settled in *colonias,* or settlements, that earlier Puerto Rican migrants had established. During the Great Migration, Spanish Harlem, a neighborhood in New York City, would become the largest and most crowded Puerto Rican neighborhood in the United States. The Puerto Rican migrants there called their new home simply *El Barrio.*

El Barrio soon became the lively center for Puerto Rican culture on the mainland. One street, 116th Street, became known as *La Marqueta,* "the market," because of the variety of shops, mostly run by Puerto Ricans as the years went by. Other Puerto Rican neighborhoods were found in the South Bronx, South Central Harlem, and Brooklyn. By 1964, nearly one out of every ten people in New York City was Puerto Rican.

Outside El Barrio and other Puerto Rican enclaves, the migrants were often subject to the same types of prejudice and discrimination that other Latino immigrants had already faced. Puerto Rican migrants were frequently left with no choice but to take low-paying, menial jobs. As a result, poverty continued to affect Puerto Ricans on the mainland much more than other Latino groups. Yet even though the wages were low compared to the pay for other jobs in the United States, most migrants from the island could still make nearly twice as much on the mainland as they could back in Puerto Rico.

# The Great Migration from Puerto Rico

As jobs in New York City became harder to come by in the 1960s and 1970s, Puerto Ricans moved to industrial areas where factory and mining jobs were plentiful. Others settled in farming areas and took work as farm laborers. They settled in Rhode Island, Connecticut, Illinois, Pennsylvania, Ohio, and Indiana. The largest Puerto Rican community outside New York City was in Chicago, Illinois.

This scene in Spanish Harlem in May 1964 was typical of Latino neighborhoods in the 1960s. Shops and stands used Spanish signs to make their customers feel at ease.

## Helping Newcomers Fit In

Like other Latino groups, the family, or *la familia,* was of primary importance to Puerto Rican migrants to the mainland. A person who decided to remain on the mainland was usually quickly joined by the rest of the family. However, as time went on and unemployment and poverty took a toll, the number of single-parent families among mainland Puerto Ricans grew. By 1980, nearly half of all Puerto Rican families with children were headed by a single parent, usually the mother.

Puerto Ricans, like other newly arrived groups of immigrants, founded mutual-aid societies to help each other in times of hardship. Many of the Puerto Rican groups were known as *hermandades,* or brotherhoods. Hermandades were often based on a person's class, region of birth in Puerto Rico, or race.

Another popular type of club was the hometown club. People joined hometown clubs to socialize with those who had migrated from the same area of Puerto Rico. They met to reminisce about the island, play cards, and plan holidays and other celebrations. The hometown clubs also helped members find jobs, temporary shelter, and emergency financial aid. In 1958, *El Congreso del Pueblo,* "the Council of Hometown Clubs," would help organize the Puerto Rican Day Parade, a tradition that continues to this day.

One of the most important Puerto Rican associations of the 1950s and 1960s was the Puerto Rican Forum, founded in New York in 1957. The group's goal was to fight the poverty that many migrants experienced. It did this by giving funding and other assistance to community organizations to help them survive and succeed.

In Puerto Rico, most people followed the Roman Catholic religion. Catholic churches on the mainland gave migrants a familiar place to go. If the Latino population was large enough in an area, migrants could attend masses in their own language. In some areas, Puerto Ricans shared their churches with people of Mexican descent. In New York, however, Catholic churches began serving mostly Puerto Ricans.

The Puerto Ricans were not the only Latino group to contribute to U.S. culture. In the coming years, new groups of immigrants and refugees would arrive in the United States and leave their own distinct mark on the nation.

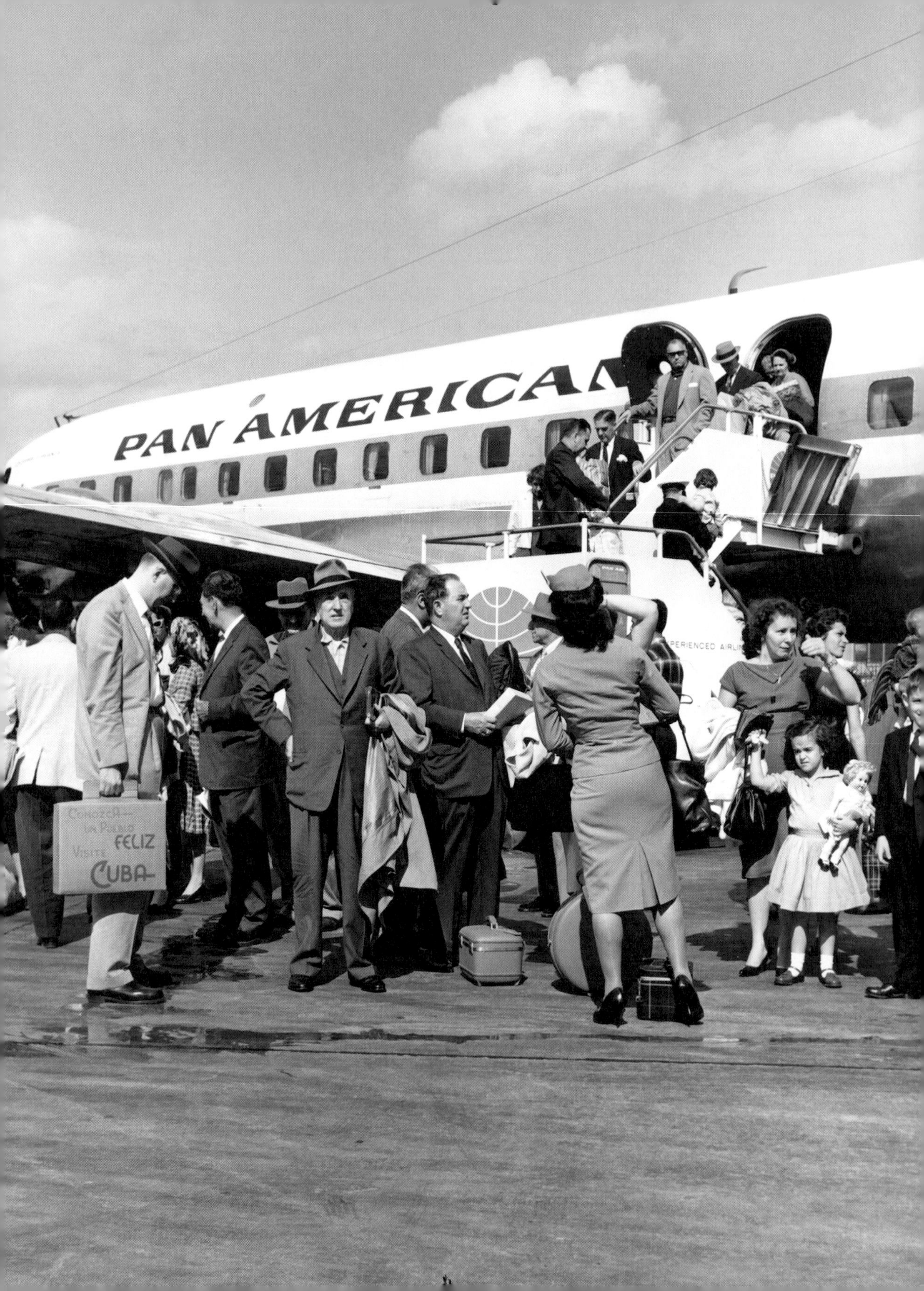
PAN AMERICAN
CONOZCA
UN PUEBLO FELIZ
VISITE
CUBA

# Latino Immigration from the Caribbean

# 5

After the United States won the Spanish-American War in 1898, Spain handed over Guam, Puerto Rico, and the Philippines to the United States. In return, Spain received $20 million. Cuba, the Spanish colony that had been at the center of the conflict, was granted its freedom. However, the United States effectively took control of the island by placing U.S. military leaders at the head of Cuba's new government.

In 1934, a Cuban general named Fulgencio Batista took control of Cuba's government and ruled the island as a corrupt dictator. He invited crime bosses from the United States to invest in Cuban land and businesses, and he brutally put down any opposition to his rule.

Although a few people in Cuba (especially U.S. businessmen and the wealthy) benefited from Batista's rule, most did not. The majority of Cubans were poor peasants and farm workers. Thousands of others were unemployed, and many had no access to schools, social services, water, or electricity. The country was ripe for a rebellion.

OPPOSITE Refugees from Havana, Cuba, arrive in Miami, Florida, on January 5, 1961, following the takeover of the Cuban government by Fidel Castro.

That rebellion came in 1959, when Fidel Castro and Argentine revolutionary Ernesto "Che" Guevara led thousands of peasants against Batista's oppressive government. The revolutionaries were successful, and Batista fled for his life to Spain.

Castro proclaimed Cuba a socialist state and named himself as leader for life. Under his rule, the Cuban government took control of most businesses and land on the island. Castro improved the quality of roads, education, and health care in Cuba, but he was still a harsh dictator. Anyone who dared to speak out against him or oppose his new government was executed or jailed without trial.

> **Fast Fact**
> Che Guevara died in 1967 while attempting to overthrow Bolivia's military government.

Batista's supporters fled the country, many of them taking shelter in Florida. Other Cubans who were unhappy with the country's new direction—especially landowners, middle-class citizens, and the wealthy—also quickly left the island. Between 1959 and 1962, more than 155,000 Cubans migrated to the United States.

Most of the Cubans in this wave of immigrants were educated and wealthy. They had the means to soon become successful in the United States. The majority of these immigrants settled in southern Florida, particularly in the city of Miami. The areas around Miami, especially Ybor City, had been home to a significant population of Cuban people since the 1830s. Before Batista's overthrow, as many as 15,000 people left Cuba each year to settle in the United States, many of them in Florida.

In the 1960s and 1970s, many Cuban immigrants settled in a section of Miami that became known as Little Havana. The heart of Little Havana was Calle Ocho, or Eighth Street. Here, Cubans could patronize grocery stores, Cuban food stands, restaurants, and other businesses that catered to the Spanish-speaking population.

Because many Cubans in Little Havana believed that their exile was only temporary, that Castro would soon be overthrown, they did not worry about learning the language of their new home. These new political refuges made sure that their children also learned or retained Spanish.

In Ybor City, Florida, Cuban Americans gather in front of a Cuban club to share the news that Cuba's president, Fulgencia Batista, had fled the island on January 1, 1959.

## Relations Worsen

In January 1961, U.S. president Dwight Eisenhower severed diplomatic relations with Cuba. Later that year, the U.S. Congress authorized an embargo, or ban on the importing and exporting of most goods to and from Cuba. In 1962, air flights between the two countries were halted.

On April 17, 1961, hundreds of Cuban exiles—armed and trained by the U.S. government—tried to take control of the island. But when the Cuban Brigada ("Brigade") landed near the Bay of Pigs in Cuba, Castro's forces were waiting. Although the United States had promised air and ground support, President John F. Kennedy withdrew all military aid at the last minute. Kennedy worried that the mission might fail or that U.S. aid to the rebels might provoke the Soviet Union to retaliate. As a result, the Bay of Pigs invasion failed miserably.

In 1962, the Soviet Union, the Cold War enemy of the United States, sent nuclear missiles to Cuba. The missiles were meant to protect the island nation from any further U.S. interference. From Cuba, the nuclear weapons could have easily reached

### The Bay of Pigs

The Cuban Brigada at the Bay of Pigs was made up mostly of young men, exiles who wanted to return to a free Cuba. Their first assault on the island was made on April 15, 1961. That day, Cuban pilots flew old World War II bombers over Cuba's air force bases, hoping to wipe out Castro's ability to launch air attacks. However, no enemy planes were destroyed, and future air strikes were canceled.

On April 17, the ground forces arrived. They fought with Castro's troops for three days before being overwhelmed. Most of the prisoners were held in Cuba until December 1962, when they were returned to Miami. Today, a monument in Little Havana memorializes the men who gave their lives in the futile effort to free their homeland.

the United States. President Kennedy threatened the Soviets with nuclear war, and after a two-week standoff, the missiles were removed.

Another wave of Cuban immigration began in 1965. That year, President Lyndon B. Johnson allowed daily flights between Cuba and Miami to resume. Cubans were given special status as refugees and allowed to immigrate in larger numbers. Between 1965 and 1972, about 257,000 Cubans left the island. The flights were ended in 1973.

The vast majority of these immigrants also chose to settle in Miami. However, their large numbers put a strain on Miami's city services. To ease the strain, the U.S. government established the U.S. Cuban Refugee Program. The goal of the program was to resettle Cubans throughout the nation. About 300,000 Cubans were resettled in New York, New Jersey, and California, but many returned to the Miami area by the early 1980s.

## The Mariel Boatlift

The third wave of Cuban immigration to the United States began in April 1980, when Castro announced that he would allow anyone who wanted to leave Cuba to do so. He also announced that Cuban exiles living in the United States could return by boat to pick up their friends and families. Thousands of islanders jumped at this chance.

The "Freedom Flotilla" left from the port of Mariel, so the mass migration from Cuba became known as the Mariel boatlift. The Cubans traveled in whatever watercraft they could find, including old rowboats and homemade rafts.

The 125,000 people who left Cuba during the boatlift were called *Marielitos,* or "those who came from Mariel." Their destination was the closest piece of U.S. soil: Key West.

Most of the new arrivals were poor, uneducated laborers. Many were black. In addition, U.S. officials believed that Castro used the boatlift as an opportunity to send not just political prisoners out of the country, but also violent criminals and the mentally ill. Sources say that about 4,000 of the total 125,000 Marielitos were such people.

During the Mariel boatlift of April 1980, a shrimp boat arrives in Key West, Florida, full of Cuban refugees.

Unfortunately, the small number of these people sent to the United States by Castro caused U.S. residents to be less accepting of all the new arrivals. Thousands of Cuban immigrants were detained in refugee tent cities and a football stadium as they awaited the government's decision on whether they would be allowed to stay in the United States. Because many of the refugees did not have families already in the United States, some were forced to spend years in the camps waiting for a U.S. citizen to sponsor them. Those who were found to have been serious criminals in Cuba were sent to jails in the United States.

Because of the poor treatment many Marielitos received, a number of groups were founded to help the new arrivals. One such group was the Cuban American Legal Defense and Education Fund, founded in 1980. The organization worked for the fair treatment of Cubans by trying to end stereotyping of Latinos. Another group that was founded shortly after the Marielitos arrived was the Cuban American National Council. Organized in 1981, the group's goal is to create support in the United States for a Castro-free Cuba.

## Immigration from the Dominican Republic

The Dominican Republic is a nation about 850 miles (1,370 km) southeast of Miami and just 80 miles (130 km) west of Puerto Rico on the island of Hispaniola. Unrest and violence plagued the country throughout its early history, and in 1916, the U.S. military occupied the nation in order to restore order and protect the Panama Canal. The Marines remained in the Dominican Republic until 1924.

In 1930, General Rafael Trujillo Molina took control of the Dominican Republic. Over the next three decades, the general turned the nation into a dictatorship. Under Trujillo's rule, few Dominicans were allowed to immigrate to the United States.

In 1961, Trujillo was assassinated. Unrest spread throughout the nation as a number of groups fought to take control of the government. After Trujillo's death, many Dominicans seized the opportunity to leave their poverty-stricken country. The number of legal immigrants to the United States jumped from 756 in 1960 to 9,504 in 1965. The number of documented arrivals from the Dominican Republic continued to grow throughout the 1970s and 1980s.

Some Dominicans immigrated illegally. They did this by going first to Puerto Rico, then to the United States. Once on the mainland, they claimed Puerto Rican—hence U.S.—citizenship. Others arrived in the United States on temporary work or tourist visas, then remained illegally past the time when they were to return. Some studies estimate that as many as 17 percent of all Dominican immigrants in the United States are undocumented.

## Dominicans in the United States

As with Puerto Rican migration, the first wave of Dominicans entering the United States was made up mostly of young men looking for work. The Dominican arrivals were generally uneducated, unskilled, and poor.

They were hired for the lowest-paying jobs in U.S. factories, as well as for service jobs that required little training. Dominicans, like other Latino groups, were also the victims of discrimination and prejudice in the workplace.

The major destinations for Dominican immigrants were manufacturing centers in the Northeast, as well as in Florida and Puerto Rico. Most of the first wave settled in the New York area and found jobs in the city's garment industry. Later Dominican immigrants chose Miami, with its large Spanish-speaking population, as a new home.

Like Puerto Rican immigrants, the Dominicans have been slow to adapt to U.S. culture. The closeness of the homeland makes return trips easy, allowing immigrants to retain their ties to their island heritage. Settling in preexisting Spanish-speaking neighborhoods has also helped the Dominicans hold on to their Latino heritage.

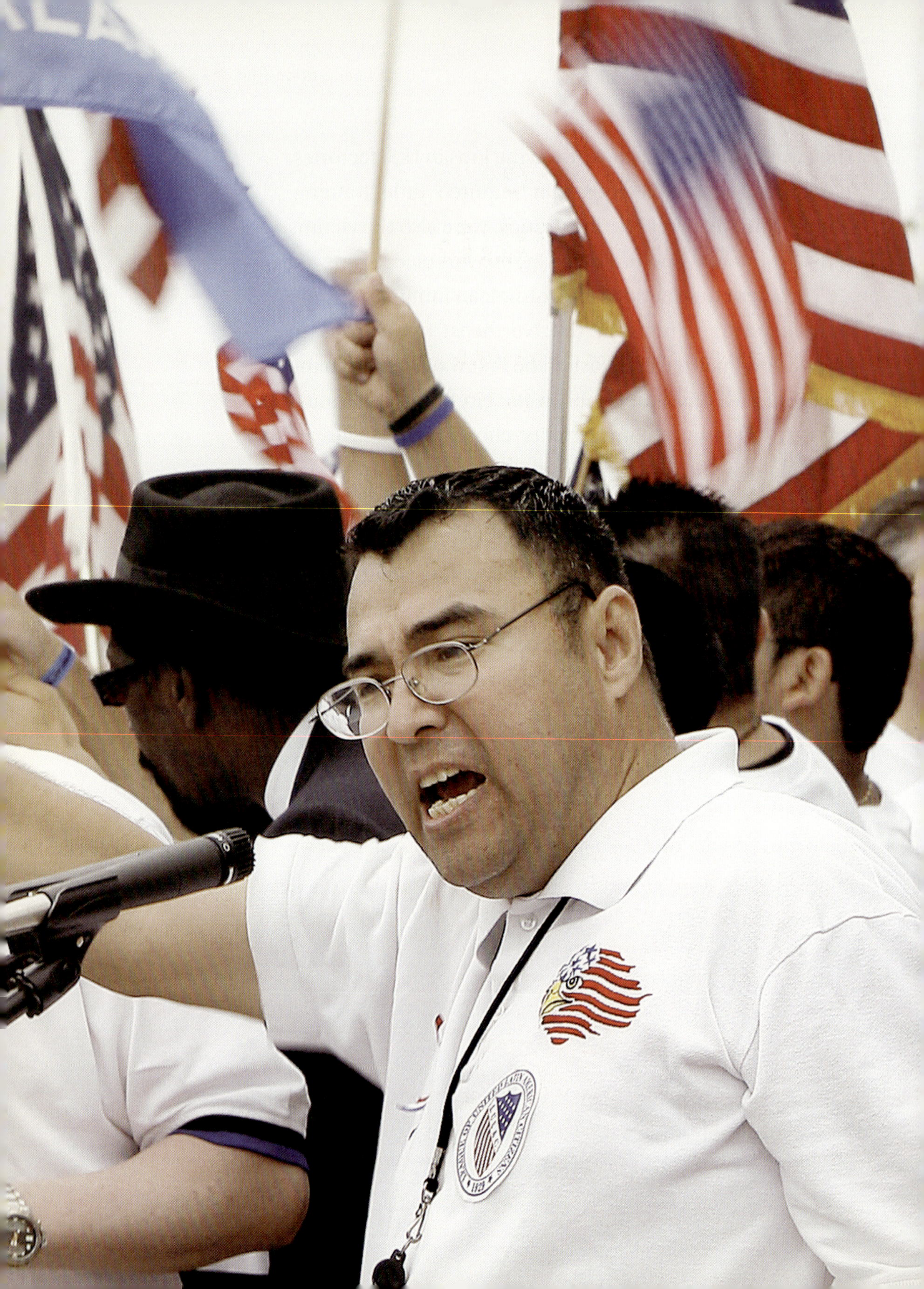

# The Struggle for Civil Rights

# 6

In the 1950s, 1960s, and early 1970s, Latino citizens across the United States began speaking out for equal treatment. During this period, dozens of Latino political, employment, civil rights, and other organizations were formed or became more active. Latino groups that worked for equal rights were known collectively as *el movimiento* ("the movement").

One way that the movement was spread was through the many Latino newspapers that appeared during the 1960s and 1970s. By the late 1970s, about 100 Spanish-language newspapers were being published across the nation. Labor unions even created their own Spanish-language or bilingual newspapers and magazines to help workers keep current with strikes, boycotts, and other labor actions. (A boycott is the organized act of not buying from or associating with a group or company in order to bring about change.)

One of the most widely read Spanish-language dailies was *La Opinión,* founded in Los Angeles in 1926 by Mexican immigrant Ignacio E. Lozano. On the East Coast,

OPPOSITE In April 2006, the struggle for civil rights continues. Victor Garcia speaks on the steps of Oklahoma's capitol at the Justice and Dignity for All Immigrants Rally.

*El Diario/La Prensa* was the most influential. This newspaper was formed when two Spanish-language papers merged in 1963. One of the original papers, *La Prensa,* had been in existence since 1913.

In the 1960s, many people of Mexican ancestry living in the United States embraced the label "Chicano," a shortened version of "Mexicano," to describe themselves and show pride in their heritage. The Chicanos' fight for fair treatment in the United States—especially in the Southwest—became known as the Chicano movement.

## Old Groups, New Groups

As U.S. society put increasing pressure on immigrants to assimilate, many Latino groups became more outspoken and active. One such group was the League of United Latin American Citizens (LULAC). Founded in 1929, LULAC's original goals were aiding Mexican Americans and other Latinos while at the same time encouraging them to adapt to life in the United States.

Beginning in the late 1940s, LULAC joined with other Latino rights groups to support lawsuits aimed at ending segregation in the United States. LULAC members also tried new, more radical tactics, such as walkouts, to achieve results. Because of these and other efforts during the civil rights era, Latino groups were eventually successful in helping end segregation in Texas and Arizona.

In addition to such groups as LULAC and the G.I. Forum, young Latino activists formed more radical associations. One such group was the *Alianza Federal de las Mercedes*

(Federal Alliance of Land Grants), founded in New Mexico in the early 1960s by Chicano activist Reies López Tijerina. The group's goal was to win back millions of acres in the Southwest—land that had been taken from Latinos when the United States took control of the region after the Mexican-American War in 1848. Once they won back their land, Alianza members hoped to create a separatist Mexican-American community. The group came to national attention in October 1966 when Tijerina and other members occupied some land in Kit Carson National Forest in New Mexico. Tijerina and five Alianza members were arrested.

In 1968, Tijerina encouraged Latinos to take part in Martin Luther King Jr.'s Poor People's March on Washington, D.C. In Washington, Tijerina made plans to carry out a citizen's arrest of certain officials back in New Mexico, including the governor. As a result, Tijerina was again arrested and tried on a variety of federal crimes. He was sentenced to five years in prison, but was released in July 1971. The Alianza existed until the 1980s, when it dissolved.

> **Fast Fact**
>
> Latino civil rights activists were inspired by the efforts of groups like the National Association for the Advancement of Colored People (NAACP) and people like Dr. Martin Luther King Jr. in their fight for equal rights for African Americans.

## Fighting for Fair Labor

For decades, Latino laborers had suffered from unfair treatment. Although some gains had been made during the 1940s, Latino laborers were still exploited by the owners of farms, mines, and factories.

In 1962, former migrant worker César Chávez and Dolores Huerta formed the National Farm Workers Association, later known as the United Farm Workers. The goal of Chávez's union was to make sure that all farm workers—many of them Latinos—were treated fairly and allowed to earn a living wage.

Starting in 1965, Chávez and his group of about 1,700 farm families organized a number of successful strikes and boycotts. The goal of these nonviolent actions was to force farm owners to negotiate with the union and to turn the spotlight on poor working conditions. The most famous of these efforts was *la Huelga* ("the Strike"), which began in 1965. That September, 800 members of Chávez's new union began picketing grape growers in Delano, California.

The strike lasted for five years. It is estimated that as many as 17 million U.S. residents took part in the grape boycott by refusing to purchase California grapes. In 1970, grape growers in the region finally signed a contract that guaranteed laborers better working conditions.

Thanks to Chávez's efforts, in 1975, California passed the California

## A Latina Activist

Dolores Huerta was born in the mining town of Dawson, New Mexico, in 1930. As a Mexican American in a California high school, Huerta experienced firsthand the racism that most Latinos in the United States suffered.

Huerta met César Chávez when she joined the CSO in 1955. In 1962, she and Chávez left the organization to found the National Farm Workers Association. Through the years, Huerta worked hard to advance the cause of agricultural laborers throughout the United States. She negotiated labor contracts, spoke to politicians on behalf of the workers, and organized strikes. Today Huerta continues to be an advocate for workers, immigrants, and women across the United States.

Labor Relations Act. The law, an important victory for farm workers, allowed secret ballots for union elections and voting rights for migrant workers and gave workers the legal right to boycott.

During the 1960s and 1970s, Latino membership in labor unions grew. Then union membership began a steep decline in 1981, with the election of Ronald Reagan as president and an employment boom.

## Fighting for a Fair Education

After World War II, Latino children began attending public schools in greater numbers than ever before. However, many Latino children were forced to attend segregated schools that focused less on academics than on assimilation and life skills. Additionally, the Latino schools were often run down, with little play space and second-rate equipment.

Children who attended public schools in the United States were encouraged or forced to speak only English. There was no recognition of Latino culture in these schools, either; only Anglo history and culture were taught and celebrated in the public schools.

The children of undocumented or migrant workers were at risk of not receiving any education at all. In some areas, the children of migrant workers were not allowed to enroll in public schools. In the early 1970s, for example, Texas school officials began prohibiting these children from attending public schools.

In the 1970s, a number of states passed laws allowing bilingual education programs. One of the first was in Dade

County, Florida, which had created a half-English, half-Spanish curriculum in the 1960s to teach the children of newly arrived Cuban immigrants. In 1968, the success of the students in the Dade County program encouraged the U.S. Congress to add a bilingual education amendment to a new education law.

At City Hall in New York City in 1967, a civil rights demonstration is held by Puerto Ricans.

In 1973 and 1978, federal laws promoted the use of bilingual and bicultural education. However, wording in the laws made it clear that the federal government wanted schools to focus principally on teaching English. Additionally, most bilingual programs were not adequately funded.

Despite some gains in the 1970s and early 1980s, the public's opinion of bilingual programs in schools began to shift. Those against bilingual education believed that students in segregated, Spanish-speaking classes suffered because they were neither hearing English spoken nor trying to speak the language for themselves. Some critics said that all students should be proficient in English in order to receive a high school diploma.

Once again, the emphasis among many public officials swung back to assimilation. Some Anglos increasingly spoke out against bilingualism, and "English only" became their rallying cry. Groups like English First were created with the goal of forcing the repeal of legislation allowing bilingual education.

## Méndez v. Westminster School District

In the 1940s, Westminster, a town in Orange County, California, was just one of many communities that ran separate—and inferior—schools for Latino children. Then, in 1945, Gonzalo Méndez and four other Mexican-American fathers (all World War II veterans) decided to fight for the right of their children to a fair education. With the help of LULAC, the men filed suit against Westminster and three other school districts.

Although the families won their court case, the school district appealed the verdict. Two years later, a U.S. appeals court put an end to school segregation in the state. The decision, called *Méndez v. Westminster School District,* was a civil rights milestone. It occurred seven years before the Supreme Court put an end to all segregation in schools throughout the country in *Brown v. Board of Education.*

# Fighting for American Values

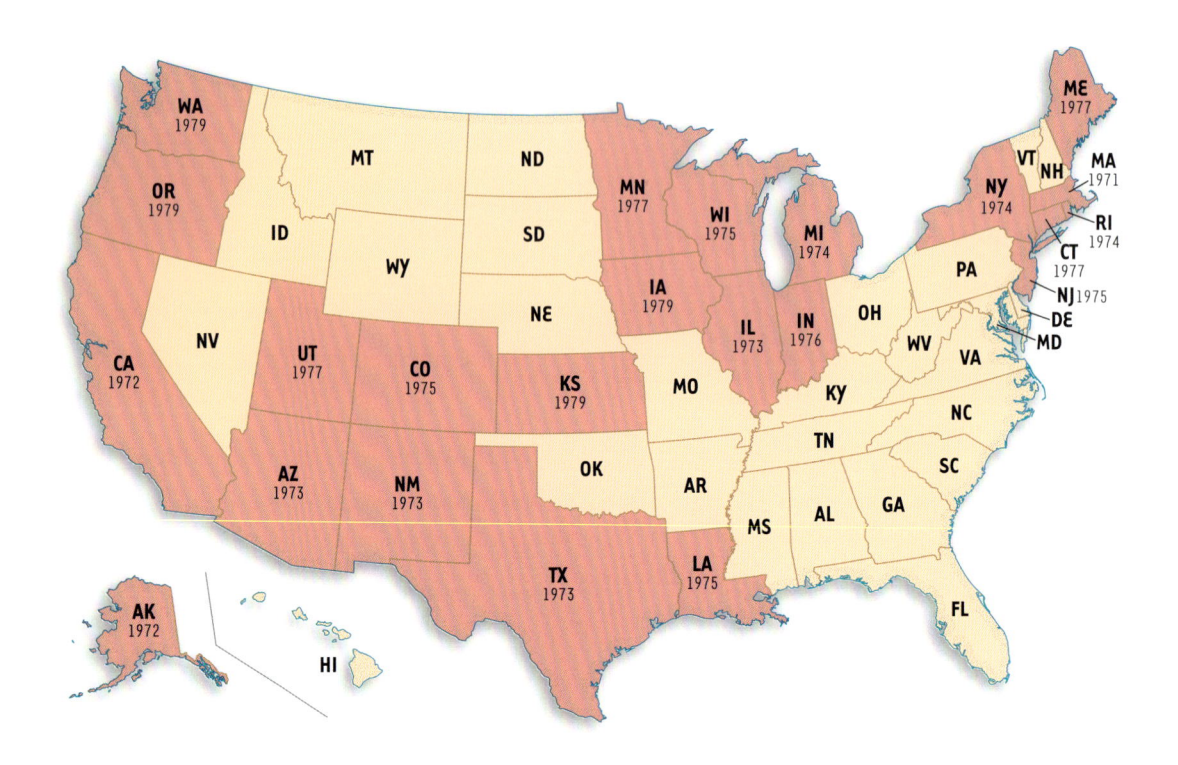

States that passed laws promoting education for non-English-speaking students are highlighted in red on the map. Each highlighted state has the date such laws were first passed there.

Many of those involved in the fight to promote bilingual and bicultural education were the young people themselves. One such group was the Brown Berets, a group formed in 1967 by teenagers living in the barrios of Los Angeles. The Brown Berets (who earned their name because of the hats they wore) acted nonviolently to force school board officials to make sure that Mexican-American culture was included in school curriculums.

Another youth group that was active during the civil rights era was the Mexican American Youth Organization (MAYO). The group was founded in 1967 by José Ángel Gutiérrez and four other young Chicano men in San Antonio. MAYO focused on such issues as equal education, workers' rights, and police brutality against Latinos. In 1970, the group shifted focus and turned its attention to politics in the Southwest.

## Puerto Rican Resistance

The 1960s was also a period of radical rebellion among Puerto Rican youth. Believing that equal rights could be won only by forceful actions, some young people turned to violence to express their frustration. In June 1966, hundreds of young Puerto Ricans in Chicago rioted against police brutality. It was one of the first Puerto Rican riots in the United States.

Other young Puerto Ricans founded their own groups. The Young Lords was one of the most militant Puerto Rican youth groups. The organization had its roots as a street gang in Chicago. In the 1960s, the group transformed itself into a self-styled "Revolutionary Political Party Fighting for the Liberation of All Oppressed People." The group also wanted an independent Puerto Rico. The Young Lords remained in existence until 1976.

The 1960s and 1970s were the high point of the Latino movement. Although such groups as the United Farm Workers continued to exist, they never had the success they enjoyed during the civil rights era. However, thanks to the efforts of these groups, Latinos were now recognized as a more cohesive force than they had been before.

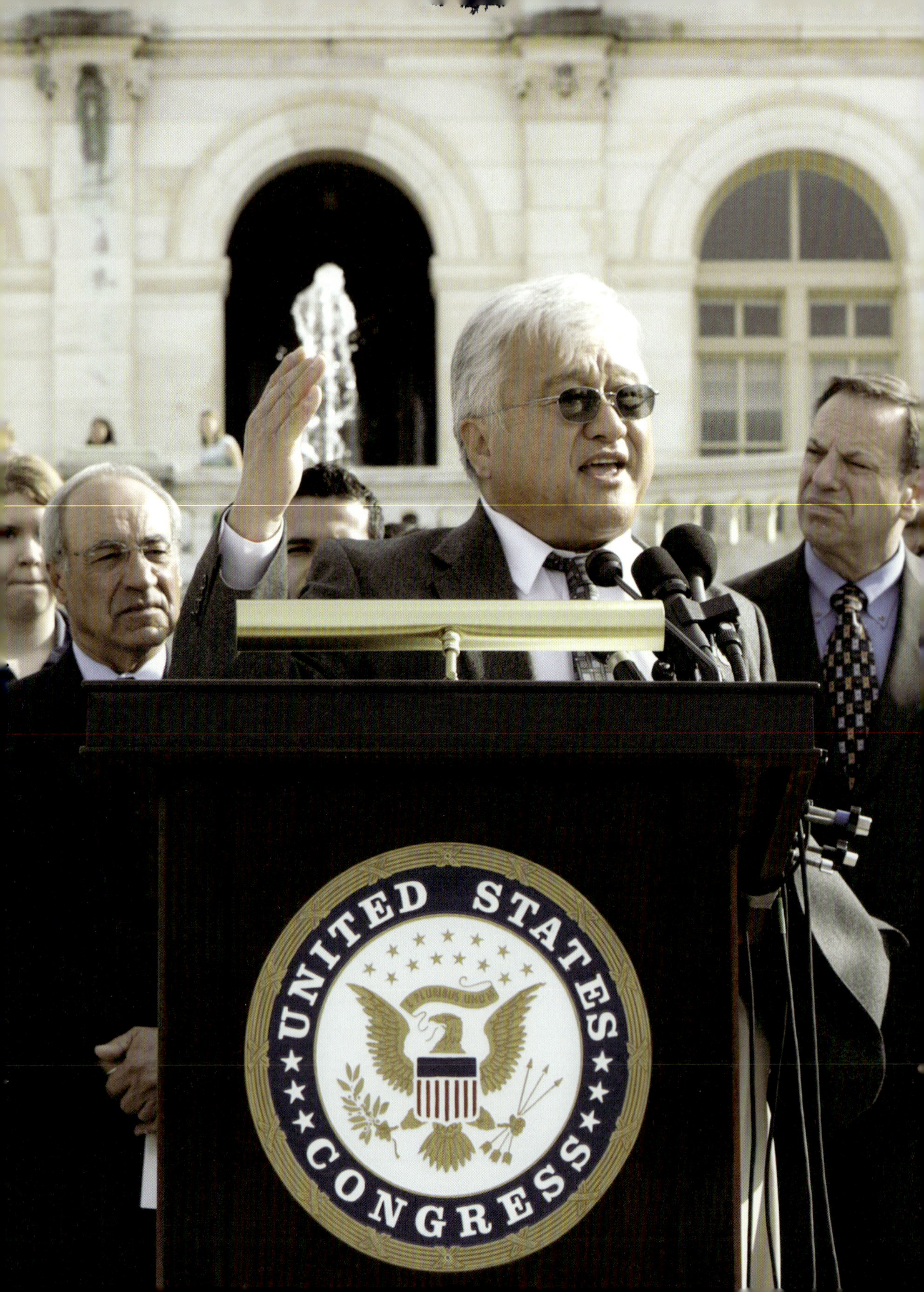
UNITED STATES
E PLURIBUS UNUM
CONGRESS

# New Political Power

7

Many Latino activists quickly realized that the best way to ensure fair treatment was to work for better political representation in community, state, and national governments. Throughout the civil rights era, groups that focused on getting Latinos elected to government positions worked hard.

In 1964, the Civil Rights Act was passed by Congress. This new set of laws, a milestone in civil rights legislation, mandated fair treatment of minorities in the workplace, in the voting booth, and in schools. The laws made it illegal for employers, school officials, and people running public places like hotels and restaurants to discriminate against anyone because of his or her race, color, religion, sex, or national origin. The Civil Rights Act provided Latinos and other minorities with the legal tools to fight prejudice and unequal treatment in the United States. Now, when employers and others violated the act, they could be sued and taken to court.

The Civil Rights Act established the first affirmative action programs in the United States. Affirmative action describes a plan or program that improves the employment

OPPOSITE   Congressional representative Mike Honda of California (center) speaks during a rally in Washington, D.C., on November 8, 2005. The Congressional Hispanic Caucus held the rally to protest the national budget, which they thought would hurt Latino Americans.

opportunities for minorities. Some affirmative action programs, for example, use quotas to ensure that certain percentages of employees are from minority groups. One such program was the Equal Employment Opportunity Commission (EEOC). In the coming years, the commission would help Latinos enter professions that had once been closed to them by working with state agencies to investigate cases of employment discrimination.

A month after the Civil Rights Act was passed, Congress passed the Economic Opportunity Act (EOA) of 1964. The goal of this law was to "eliminate . . . poverty in the midst of plenty in this Nation by opening to everyone the opportunity for education and training, the opportunity to work, and the opportunity to live in decency and dignity." The act aided Latinos by creating hundreds of public programs that provided worker training, employment assistance, youth assistance, and health and legal services in communities around the nation. Many of these programs still exist today. For example, the Job Corps helps poor youth between the ages of 16 and 21 find work, and Volunteers in Service to America (VISTA) enables people to volunteer for community service projects to help end poverty. The EOA also set up a system to monitor employment practices throughout the nation.

Shortly after the EOA was passed, LULAC and the G.I. Forum worked together to create a program called Jobs for Progress, more commonly known as SER. The letters S-E-R stand for service, employment, and redevelopment. Ser is

### Fast Fact

Since VISTA was founded in 1965, more than 120,000 people in the United States have volunteered with the organization.

also the Spanish word for "to be." SER started off as a job placement service and then started offering skills training and other employment services to Latinos in the Southwest. In 1972, SER became a part of the Department of Labor.

In September 1965, President Johnson issued an executive decision that enforced affirmative action. Johnson's decision was just one part of his War on Poverty, a series of bills and acts that were intended to end poverty in the United States. The government's support of affirmative action, however, was controversial. Many critics claimed that, because of quotas and other affirmative action policies, women and minorities were hired for jobs instead of white men who were better qualified. In response, President Johnson pointed out, "You do not take a person who, for years, has been hobbled by chains and liberate him, bring him up to the starting line of a race and then say you are free to compete with all the others, and still just believe that you have been completely fair."

## Latino Political Organizations

In the late 1960s, Latinos in the Southwest had little political representation, despite the large Latino population in the region. Most of the local, state, and federal politicians were Anglos. Some of the first Latino organizations that tried to change this situation were Unity Leagues in California. Not only did these groups register voters, they also supported Latino candidates, pushed for fair education, challenged school segregation, and helped Latinos in need.

Fighting for American Values

The Mexican American Political Association (MAPA) joined other groups at this rally in December 2003 protesting, among other things, the repeal of a law allowing immigrants to have driver's licenses.

Other groups focused exclusively on politics. These organizations included the Mexican American Political Association (MAPA) in California, the Political Association of Spanish-Speaking Organizations (PASSO) in Texas, and the American Coordinating Council for Political Education (ACCPE) in Arizona. These groups usually supported Democratic Party candidates because this party seemed more willing than the Republican Party to support Latino civil rights efforts.

Soon after its founding in early 1960, MAPA helped a Latino to a judgeship in Los Angeles. The group also sponsored many Viva Kennedy campaign clubs in California, to support presidential candidate John F. Kennedy. PASSO, founded in late 1960, had its greatest success in 1962 and 1963 in Crystal City, Texas. Here, PASSO members joined with the Teamsters Union to help Mexican Americans win all five seats on the city's council. This was the first time such a victory had been achieved in South Texas, and Latinos led the government for the next two years. The ACCPE was founded in 1960 in order to elect a Mexican-American principal to one of Phoenix's elementary schools. Mexican-American attorneys founded the Mexican Legal Defense and Education Fund (MALDEF) in San Antonio. MALDEF, modeled after the NAACP, used the U.S. legal and political systems to protect Latino rights. It took cases to court that involved inequity in education, employment, and police treatment. Beginning in the early 1970s, the group won a number of important decisions. In 1982, for example, it was instrumental in a decision that forced the Houston Independent School District to allow the children of undocumented workers to enroll in school.

## A Fighter for Civil Rights

One of the founders of MALDEF was Mario G. Obledo, a Mexican-American lawyer from Texas. In 1972, Obledo also helped found La Raza National Lawyers Association in California to represent Latino attorneys, judges, and others involved in the legal system. Today, the group is known as the Hispanic National Bar Association (HNBA) and represents more than 25,000 Latinos. In 1998, Obledo was awarded the Presidential Medal of Freedom, the highest civilian honor in the United States, in recognition of his lifelong fight for Latino civil rights.

Fighting for American Values

An election official in Idaho in 2003 shows off a bilingual ballot that is part of the *Yo Voto* (I Vote) campaign to encourage Latinos to exercise their right to vote.

In 1974, MALDEF initiated the Chicana Rights Project. The goal of this project was to protect Mexican-American women from discrimination. MALDEF was also active in challenging unfair voting practices throughout the 1970s. Between 1974 and 1984, the organization filed 88 lawsuits in an effort to allow all Mexican Americans access to the voting booth.

Another important political organization founded around the same time as MALDEF was the Southwest Voter Registration and Education Project. This group held voter registration drives throughout the Southwest region, resulting in thousands of Latinos registering to vote. The group also worked with MALDEF to file suit when it felt that Latino voting rights were being violated.

In New York in 1970, a court case brought by a Puerto Rican group ensured that all ballots in the state were bilingual. The same year, MALDEF worked to have the Voting Rights Act, first passed in 1965, amended to allow Latinos and other minorities to fully participate in the voting process. In 1975, the act was again amended to permanently ban literacy tests as a voting requirement and make bilingual ballots mandatory in some parts of the nation. In 1982, Congress once again amended the Voting Rights Act. The new changes made it illegal for any state or community within a state to create laws that would result in minorities being denied the right to vote.

In 1976, members of the Congressional Hispanic Caucus met for the first time. This group of 12 Latino members of Congress, both Democrats and Republicans, focused on making sure that Latino issues were heard and addressed. Over the years, the bipartisan group has served as a watchdog for congressional, executive, and judicial actions.

## A Latino Political Party

In the past, Latinos (with the exception of Cubans) had helped elect Democrats to office in the belief that they would aid the Latino community. However, many of these candidates disappointed Latinos by failing to follow through on their campaign promises. In January 1970,

## Romana Acosta Bañuelos

Romana Acosta Bañuelos (1925– ) was a victim of anti-Mexican sentiment during the Great Depression. In 1931, she and her family were repatriated to Mexico, a place that was foreign to Bañuelos.

Bañuelos returned to the United States when she was 19 years old, making her home in Los Angeles. Two years later, she started a tortilla factory, which she eventually turned into a million-dollar business. She also helped organize the Pan American National Bank in Los Angeles, the only bank owned and operated by Mexican Americans. In 1971, President Richard M. Nixon appointed Bañuelos as the first Chicana treasurer of the United States. She served until 1974.

---

MAYO founder José Ángel Gutiérrez decided that the time had come to unite Latinos in Texas under a new party banner. He and about 300 other Mexican Americans joined together to found *La Raza Unida* (the United People) Party (LRUP), the first Latino political party in the United States.

The party first focused its attention on three communities in South Texas that had large Mexican populations but little Latino representation in town government. LRUP managed to place a number of its Latino candidates on the ballot in these cities, and in April, 15 Latino Americans were elected to office. In two communities, the LRUP candidates won a majority on the council and the school board. Two of LRUP's candidates were elected mayor of their cities.

In Crystal City, where LRUP candidates had won a majority of seats on the school board, the new board began a policy of hiring more Mexican-American teachers. They also began a free-lunch program for needy students. In addition, Mexican-American studies were made a part of the city schools' curriculum.

After the win, LRUP branches popped up throughout the Southwest and West. Some party members even hoped to take the LRUP national and make it a major third party. However, fighting about the party's direction, some significant failures during elections, and loss of membership led to the LRUP's downfall in the late 1970s.

Despite the failure of LRUP to live up to its founders' hopes, the number of Latinos in Congress continued to grow—though very slowly. In 1981, for example, there were only six Latinos in Congress. However, Latinos and Latinas were being selected for government appointments. One was Linda Chavez, placed on the Civil Rights Commission by President Ronald Reagan in 1983.

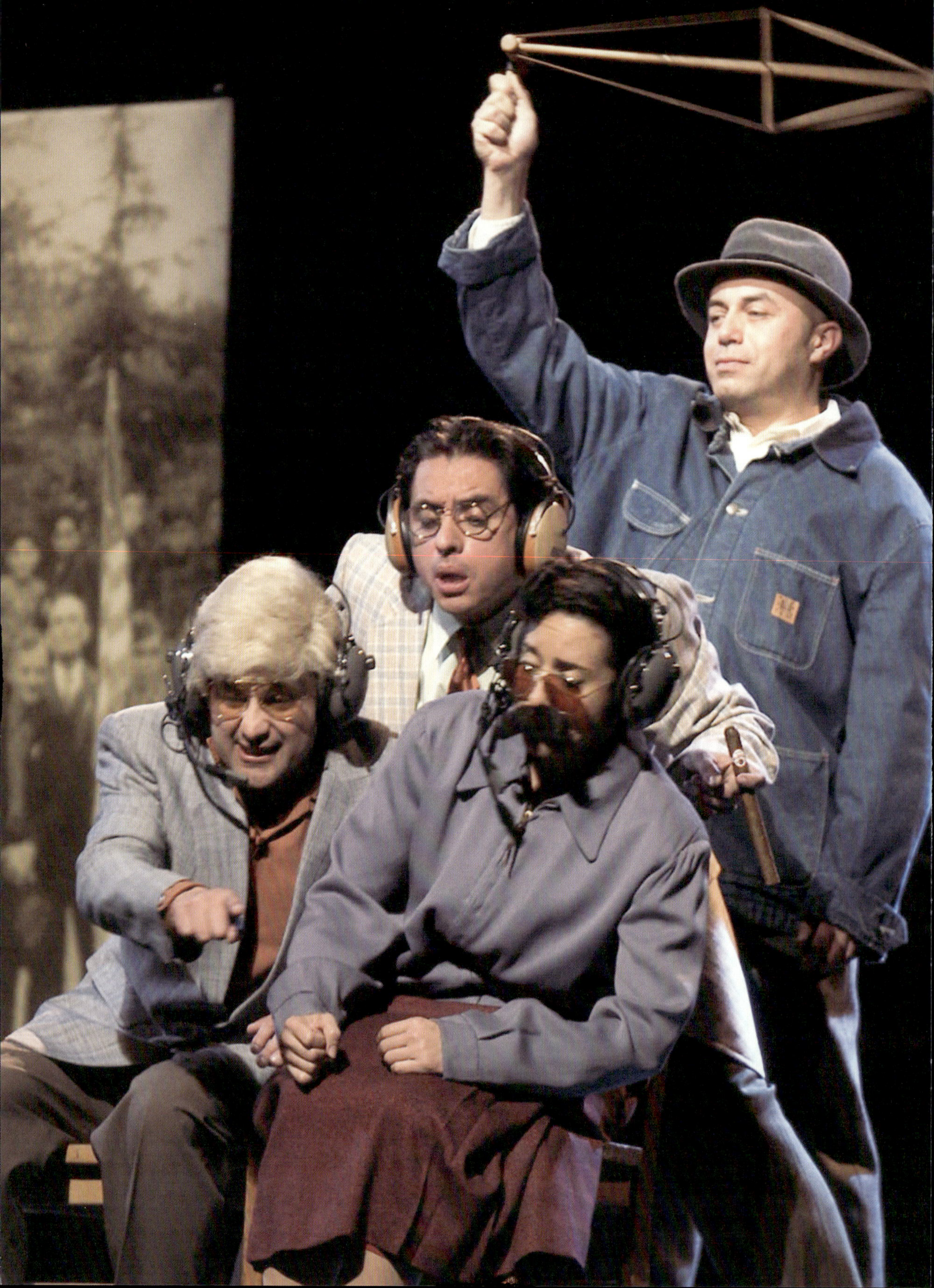

# A Growing Cultural Influence

# 8

Beginning in the 1960s, Latinos were more visible in many areas of U.S. culture. They acted in movies and on TV shows. They created art, wrote books and poetry, and made popular music. Latino sports stars—especially in baseball—also brought attention to the contributions Latinos make every day in the United States.

In the 1970s, Latino media also expanded. During that decade, more than 500 radio stations and 70 television stations included Spanish-language programming. The growth would continue into the 1980s.

## Movies

The civil rights movement offered the movie industry some images of which Latinos could be proud. However, the same period saw a continuation of the old stereotypes of Latinos as lazy, bumbling "greasers," evil banditos, hot-blooded lovers, and dark ladies. Most of the Latino roles in movies continued to be played by Anglo actors.

OPPOSITE The Latino comedy group Culture Clash puts on the play *Chavez Ravine* in March 2004 at the U.S. Comedy Arts Festival in Aspen, Colorado.

One example of both positive and negative portrayals of Latinos was *West Side Story* (1961). The movie featured a star-crossed love story between a Latino teen and her Anglo boyfriend. The story also featured the rivalry between two youth gangs, one Puerto Rican and one Anglo.

Many Latinos felt the movie wrongly portrayed them as favoring a violent, gang lifestyle. Latino gang portrayals did increase after the movie's success. *West Side Story* actually featured only one Latino actor in a major role: Rita Moreno, as the girlfriend of a gang member.

Puerto Rican actress Rita Moreno won an Academy Award for her role in the movie *West Side Story* in 1961.

In the late 1960s and the 1970s, the film industry was targeted by civil rights groups. LULAC, MALDEF, and other groups began pushing for more Latinos to be included. In 1969, actor Ricardo Montalbán helped form NOSOTROS, a group that protested the stereotypical roles that Latinos were given. The group also worked to improve the image of Latinos that Hollywood portrayed.

Despite the difficulties of becoming a star in Hollywood, a number of Latino actors found success on the silver screen during the 1960s and 1970s. These talented Latinos included Hector Elizondo, Rita Moreno, Edward James Olmos, Anthony Quinn, Martin Sheen, and Raquel Welch.

## Creating Latino Cinema

In the the late 1970s, a group of Latinos banded together to form the Los Angeles Chicano Cinema Coalition. The organization's goal was to create Chicano films that told the story of Latinos during the civil rights movement, focusing on social justice for all Latinos.

Long before this mainland effort to make Latino cinema, the island of Puerto Rico had its own film industry. Although the industry dated from the early 1900s, the first large movie company in Puerto Rico was founded in 1951. Viguié Film Productions made commercial and documentary films, both for the government and private companies. In 1974, it became Guastella Film Producers.

In 1976, the first Chicano Film Festival in the United States took place in San Antonio. The festival's goal was to provide a place for Latino filmmakers to screen their movies. Today, the film festival—now called the San Antonio Cinefestival—continues to be held each year in June. It is the oldest and largest such showcase for Latino filmmakers in the United States.

# Television

In the 1960s and 1970s, more Latino characters were included on television programs. Unfortunately, most of the characters were stereotypes that reinforced the prejudices that many Anglos held about Latinos. Latinos routinely appeared on police dramas as gang members and criminals. On TV westerns, Latinos often appeared as the wicked banditos.

During the 1970s, a number of Latino actors earned fame on television. They included Puerto Rican comedian Freddie Prinze, who starred in *Chico and the Man,* and Puerto Rican actor Erik (Enrique) Estrada, who starred in the motorcycle cop drama *CHiPS*. Ricardo Montalbán, founder of NOSOTROS, got the lead role in *Fantasy Island*. Latinas also had success in television, but almost always as Anglo characters. They included Lynda Carter *(Wonder Woman),* Catherine Bach *(The Dukes of Hazzard),* and Victoria Principal *(Dallas)*.

It was not just the television programs that portrayed Latino stereotypes. Beginning in 1967, Latinos watching television were treated to ads featuring the Frito Bandito, a chubby, mustachioed Mexican bandit. After protests from the Mexican-American community, the bandito was pulled from the chip ads in 1970. Another stereotyped selling tool was Chiquita Banana, a Latina spitfire in the guise of a banana with a big fruit hat. "Miss Chiquita," as the character was called, has most recently been updated from a banana to a live female spokesperson.

Some children's shows also began including a Latino flavor. *Sesame Street* went on the air in 1969. The *Sesame*

*Street* writers celebrated diversity, creating roles for Latinos and inserting Spanish words and phrases into shows. In 1971, the Latino character Luis made his debut. Soon, he was joined by Maria, and the two often spoke Spanish together. *Sesame Street* was the first national preschool program to teach bilingualism. In 1972, Mexico began producing its own Spanish-language version of *Sesame Street,* called *Plaza Sésamo.* The show was also broadcast to Spanish-speaking households in the United States.

In 1961, the first Spanish-language TV network was founded. Called the Spanish International Network (SIN), the new network created Spanish-language programming while selling advertising to keep the network afloat. In the coming years, SIN would remain the most powerful and widely broadcast Spanish network. It was even the first major network in the United States to provide satellite broadcasting of programs to its affiliates. Today, SIN is known as Univision.

## Latino Theater

In 1965, playwright Luis Valdez founded *El Teatro Campesino,* the Farmworkers' Theater. The company was a branch of César Chavez's United Farm Workers that traveled throughout the Southwest, motivating Latino workers to fight for their civil rights. In the early 1970s, El Teatro Campesino launched a Chicano grass-roots theater movement. In communities throughout the West and Southwest, Latinos began staging productions in churches, universities, schools, and other community centers. Many of the productions were one-act plays that focused on the discrimination and prejudice directed at Mexican Americans. Unfortunately, many of these drama groups would not outlast the 1970s.

New York was a vibrant center for Latino theater. One of the most famous theater companies was Miriam Colón's Puerto Rican Traveling Theatre (PRTT), founded in 1967. Colón was a Puerto Rican who came to the mainland in 1954. The mobile theater she founded performed Spanish and English plays in the streets of New York's barrios. The PRTT, which spurred the founding of other Latino theater companies, is still going strong today.

Two well-known Puerto Rican theater actors of the time were Raúl Juliá and Rita Moreno. Born in 1940, Juliá got his start with the PRTT. He was nominated for several awards for his work in Broadway plays. To children, Juliá was better known for playing Gomez Addams in the 1991 movie, *The Addams Family*. Rita Moreno, born in 1931, was one of the first Puerto Rican performers to find success on the New York stage. She won an Oscar for her role in the movie *West Side Story*.

## Latino Art

During the 1970s, Latino art in the form of colorful murals earned national attention. The muralist movement started because Latino artists wanted to make art that was accessible to all Latinos. Modeling their art after great Mexican artists of the 1920s to the 1950s, the artists created a sort of living museum in the barrios of the West and Southwest. Using both vibrant colors and stark blacks and whites, they painted huge pictures on the sides of buildings, in alleys, and many other places. Their murals served as a form of political protest and statement. Murals like *History and Heroes, History of the Mexican American Worker,* and *La Raza Cósmica* showed people and symbols from Latino history.

In Chicano Park in San Diego, California, freeway abutments painted with murals describing Chicano life and culture are shown in April 2000.

Two of the most important Latino muralists were Ernesto Palomino and Carlos Almaraz. Palomino is a Mexican-American artist born in Fresno, California, in 1933. He created murals in California communities in the 1970s. Almaraz, born in Mexico in 1941, moved to Chicago and then Los Angeles when he was young. He painted murals throughout the 1970s and was part of a well-known group of Latino artists who came to be known as *los Four.*

Female Mexican-American artists also flourished in California at this time. Patricia Rodríguez was one well-known muralist during the 1970s. She organized the *Mujeres Muralistas* ("*Women* Muralists"), a group of four female painters that created murals between 1972 and 1977.

## Latino Literature

During the civil rights era in the 1960s, Latino poetry was a favorite literary form. Poems were often read at meetings, boycotts, and protest marches to inspire others to action and solidarity.

Latino literary magazines began featuring Latino literature in Spanish and English. One such magazine was *El Grito (The Shout),* first published in 1967 by a group of professors at the University of California. In 1971, *El Grito* published *Bless Me, Ultima,* a novel by Mexican-American writer Rudolfo Anaya. The novel won a number of important awards, and today, Anaya is considered the father of modern Chicano literature. Unfortunately, most of the Latino literary magazines disappeared by the late 1970s.

---

### I Am Joaquín

One of the most important poems to come out of the civil rights era was *I Am Joaquín/Yo Soy Joaquín*. The poem was written by Rudolfo "Corky" González, a Latino rights activist from Colorado. Published in bilingual form, the poem focuses on the history of Mexican Americans, their struggle, and their resolve to overcome discrimination and other difficulties. The poem was read aloud at civil rights rallies and meetings. Theater companies performed the poem as street theater. Handwritten copies were passed from person to person, slowly spreading its message across the nation. In 1967, *I Am Joaquín/Yo Soy Joaquín* was turned into a movie, considered the first Chicano film.

Important Latino writers include Miguel Piñero and Nicholasa Mohr. Piñero, born in Puerto Rico in 1946, moved with his family to New York when he was just four. By the time he was 13, he had served time in a juvenile detention center. His first play, a prison drama called *Short Eyes,* was performed on Broadway and won several awards, including Play of the Year in 1974.

Nicholasa Mohr's parents migrated to New York City from Puerto Rico during World War II. Mohr grew up in the Bronx, eventually attending art school in Brooklyn. In 1974, she wrote her first children's book, *Nilda.* The book described what life was like for a 10-year-old Puerto Rican girl in New York. It received several awards.

## Music

Music has always been an important part of Latino culture. One popular type of music was created by *orquestas*. At the turn of the century, these bands, complete with violins and guitars, played at weddings, birthday parties, parades, and other public events. Later, orquestas grew to also include saxophones, trombones, trumpets, drums, and keyboards. Orquestas varied in size from four to twenty musicians.

Orquesta music was most popular in the 1960s and 1970s in Texas. Successful orquestas often played boogie, salsa, jazz, and rock 'n' roll—sometimes in the same piece of music. These mixed-genre songs became known as *La Onda Chicana,* or "the Chicano Wave." The popularity of orquestas declined in the mid-1980s.

Another style of music that remained popular among Latinos was the *corrido,* a type of song first developed in the 1920s by Latinos living in the Southwest. Corridos used both sadness and humor to describe the difficulties of being Latino. In the 1970s and 1980s, the ballads became more reactionary, describing discrimination, important events, crime against Latinos, and much more.

One corrido described the case of Félix Longoria, the World War II soldier killed in action who was refused burial services at a local funeral parlor because of his ethnicity. The song, *Discriminación,* included the following verse:

> *When the body of the soldier*
> *arrived with his next-of-kin,*
> *The mortuary in his hometown*
> *denied him a funeral.*
> *That is discrimination*
> *against a poor human being;*
> *not even in a cemetery*
> *do they allow a Mexican.*

Another type of popular Latino music was *música norteña,* also called *conjunto* by Mexicans in Texas. Conjunto first developed in the 1920s as a sort of polka-like folk music, complete with accordions and guitars. At first, the music was mainly popular with rural, working-class Latinos in the Southwest. After World War II, however, conjunto's popularity spread around the nation to all people. Today, it remains a symbol of the Chicano working class and those who embrace their Mexican culture.

Perhaps one of the best-known types of Latino music is salsa, which means "sauce" in Spanish. Like some Latino sauces, salsa is a hot and spicy rhythm that first came to popularity in the 1970s. Salsa has its roots in music from Cuba, Puerto Rico, and the Dominican Republic. It began as a combination of African music, brought to the region by slaves, and Spanish music, brought to the region by the Spanish conquerors.

In the United States, two people became known as the king and queen of salsa: Tito Puente and Celia Cruz. Puente, born in Spanish Harlem in 1923, formed his first orchestra in 1947. He was best known for playing the timbales (a type of drum), but he could play many other instruments. Celia Cruz, born in 1925, immigrated to the United States from Cuba after Castro's takeover in 1959. She teamed up with Tito Puente and helped popularize salsa music across the United States.

Celia Cruz (left) and Tito Puente (center) perform with an all-star band at a sold-out Madison Square Garden in New York City in 1994.

Beginning in the 1950s and 1960s, Latino rhythms began to get air time on Anglo stations. Ritchie Valens had a hit with a traditional Mexican song, "La Bamba." Later, Joe Cuba became famous for his song "Bang Bang." In the 1950s, such U.S. artists as Fats Domino and Bo Diddley started to include Latino rhythms in their music. The 1960s and 1970s marked the beginning of the successful careers of Trini Lopez, José Feliciano, and Carlos Santana.

## Latinos and Baseball

Baseball was introduced to Cuba in the 1860s, when Latino students returned to the island after studying in the United States. In 1878, just seven years after the National Baseball Association was founded in the United States, Cuba started its first professional baseball league.

In 1946, the first pro baseball league in Mexico was founded. The league fell apart in 1953, but was reformed two years later. Today, the Mexican Central League is a Triple-A league.

In 1947, Jackie Robinson became the first African-American player in the major leagues, opening the door for dark-skinned Latino players. Latinos quickly showed that they were as good as—or better than—many Anglo players. Important Latino major league players during the 1950s, 1960s, and 1970s include Hall of Famers Luis Aparicio, Roberto Clemente, and Juan Marichal. Other Latinos who made an impact on the game since World War II include Rod Carew, Orlando Cepeda, Dave Concepción, Keith Hernández, and Tony Oliva.

## Latinos in Other Sports

Another sport in which Latinos excelled was boxing. Lightweight Carlos Ortiz won the world boxing title in 1962, becoming the second Puerto Rican to do so (after Sixto Escobar). In 1965, medium heavyweight José Luis Torres became the third Puerto Rican boxer to win a title. In 1969 and 1972, Mexican-American Armando Ramos won the world lightweight title.

In the 1960s and 1970s, Rosemary Casals and Richard "Pancho" Gonzalez left their mark on the game of tennis. In the 1960s, Juan "Chi Chi" Rodriguez went from caddying in his native Puerto Rico to becoming a hugely successful golfer. Mexican-American Lee Treviño, most active during the 1970s, also got his start in golfing by working as a caddy. In the late 1970s and early 1980s, Mexican-American Nancy López was famous in women's golf.

Perhaps one of the best-known Latino athletes of the 1970s was football star Jim Plunkett. Plunkett won the 1970 Heisman Trophy, an honor that is given to the top college football player each year. In 1980 and 1983, Plunkett led the Oakland Raiders to victory in the Super Bowl.

During the decades after World War II, Latinos came a long way. They fought hard to win better treatment in the workplace, in schools, and other sectors of society. Mexicans continued to migrate to the United States and other Latino groups—Cubans, Puerto Ricans, and Dominicans—joined them in increasing numbers. In the coming years, Latino Americans would continue to make advances and play a more visible and vital role in U.S. culture.

# Timeline

| | |
|---|---|
| 1941 | The United States enters World War II. |
| 1942 | The United States starts the bracero program. |
| 1943 | Latinos in Los Angeles are targeted for random beatings by sailors and soldiers during the zoot suit riots. |
| 1945 | World War II ends. |
| 1948 | The American G.I. Forum is founded to fight discrimination against Latinos. Puerto Ricans elect their first governor, Luis Muñoz Marín. |
| 1950 | The U.S. government begins a repatriation program to round up and deport Mexicans working illegally in the United States. |
| 1952 | Puerto Ricans approve a new constitution for the island and the island's new status as a commonwealth. |
| 1962 | The Cuban missile crisis raises tensions between the Soviet Union, Cuba, and the United States. César Chávez founds the National Farm Workers Association, later known as the United Farm Workers. |
| 1964 | Congress passes the Civil Rights Act, mandating the fair treatment of minorities. |
| 1965 | Congress passes the Immigration and Nationality Act to limit immigration from the Western Hemisphere. Mexico begins the maquiladora program to provide jobs for former braceros. |
| 1968 | Congress passes a bilingual education amendment as part of a new education law. |
| 1970 | Mexican Americans found La Raza Unida (the United People) Party, the first Latino political party in the United States. |
| 1982 | Amendments to the Voting Rights Act of 1965 make it illegal for any state or community within a state to create laws that would result in minorities being denied the right to vote. |

# Glossary

**assimilate**  To fit into a new society or culture.

**barrio**  A Latino neighborhood.

**bilingual education**  Teaching Spanish-speaking children in both Spanish and English during their first few years in school.

**braceros**  Mexican laborers who were transported into the United States to work.

**colonia**  A town or community founded by Latino workers.

**communism**  A system of government in which all property is owned by the state and shared by all citizens.

**Foraker Act**  An act passed in 1900 that organized Puerto Rico's political system and created the position of resident commissioner to the U.S. Congress.

**hermandad**  A Puerto Rican mutual-aid society.

**Immigration and Naturalization Service (INS)**  A government agency that oversaw immigration in the United States from 1891 to 2003.

**independentista**  A person who favored Puerto Rican independence.

**Latin America**  The countries of the Western Hemisphere south of the United States, especially those in which the main language is Spanish.

**mestizo**  A person with both Spanish and American Indian ancestry.

**repatriate**  To send people back to their country of origin.

**socialism**  A political system in which large businesses are owned and controlled by the government for the benefit of all citizens.

**strike**  The organized act of stopping work in order to force an employer to improve working conditions.

# Further Reading

## Books

Cockcroft, James D., and Jane Canning. *Latino Visions: Contemporary Chicano, Puerto Rican, and Cuban-American Art.* New York: Franklin Watts, 2000.

Cofer, Judith Ortiz. *Riding Low through the Streets of Gold: Latino Literature for Young Adults.* Houston, TX: Arte Público Press, 2004.

Day, Frances Ann. *Latina and Latino Voices in Literature for Children and Teenagers.* Westport, CT: Greenwood Press, 2003.

Ford, Carin T. *Roberto Clemente: Baseball Legend.* Berkeley Heights, NJ: Enslow, 2005.

Marcovitz, Hal. *César Chávez.* New York: Chelsea House, 2003.

Winter, Jonah. *¡Béisbol! Latino Baseball Pioneers and Legends.* New York: Lee & Low, 2001.

## Web Sites

East Harlem, A Historical Perspective, http://www.eastharlemtourism.org/history.htm

The Handbook of Texas Online, http://www.tsha.utexas.edu/handbook/online/

Puerto Rico at the Dawn of the Modern Age, http://memory.loc.gov/ammem/collections/puertorico/index.html

About PRTT, http://www.prtt.org/about.html

# Bibliography

### Books

Davis, Mike. *Magical Urbanism: Latinos Reinvent the U.S. City.* New York: Verso, 2000.

Gutiérrez, David, ed. *The Columbia History of Latinos in the United States Since 1960.* New York: Columbia University Press, 2004.

Rosales, Francisco Arturo. *Testimonio: A Documentary History of the Mexican American Struggle for Civil Rights.* Houston, Tex.: Arte Público Press, 2000.

Ruiz, Vicki L., and Virginia Sánchez Korrol. *Latina Legacies: Identity, Biography, and Community.* New York: Oxford University Press, 2005.

Suro, Roberto. *Strangers Among Us: How Latino Immigration Is Transforming America.* New York: Alfred A. Knopf, 1998.

### Web Sites

California Digital Library. "The Online Archive of California (OAC)." URL: http://oac.cdlib.org/. Downloaded on August 4, 2006.

Digital History. "Mexican American Voices." URL: http://www.digitalhistory.uh.edu/mexican_voices/mexican_voices.cfm. Downloaded on August 4, 2006.

Manuel Álvarez-Rivera. "Elections in Puerto Rico." URL: http://electionspuertorico.org/home_en.html. Downloaded on August 4, 2006.

Sin Fronteras. "The Farmworkers Website." URL: www.farmworkers.org. Downloaded on August 4, 2006.

# Index

**Note:** Page numbers in *italics* indicate photographs or illustrations. Page numbers followed by m indicate maps. Page numbers followed by g indicate glossary entries. Page numbers in **bold-face** indicate box features.

### A

affirmative action 75–77
African Americans **67**
agriculture
    bracero program 26, 37
    farm workers 1, 14, *vi*
    workers' rights 26–29, *27*, **28**
*Alianza Federal de las Mercedes* (Federal Alliance of Land Grants) 66–67
Almaraz, Carlos 91
American Coordinating Council for Political Education (ACCPE) 78, 79
American G.I. Forum 23
American Indians **5**, 9
Anaya, Rudolf 92
Aparicio, Luis 96
Arizona 78, 79
Arnaz, Desi 41–42, *42*
art, Latino 90–92, *91*
assimilate 36, 38, 40–42, 71, 99g
awards, military **15**, 31–32

### B

Bach, Catherine 88
Balboa, Vasco Núñez de 9
Ball, Lucille 42, *42*
Bañuelos, Romana Acosta **82**
barrio 35, 36, 99g. *See also* Spanish Harlem
baseball, Latinos in 85, 96
Batista, Fulgencio (Cuban dictator) 55–56, 57
Bay of Pigs invasion, Cuba 58, **58**
bilingual ballots 80, 81
bilingual education 69–72, 99g
*Bless Me, Ultima* (Anaya) 92
*Board of Education, Brown v.* **71**
boxing 97
boycott 65
bracero program **18**, 18–19, *19*, 26
braceros 26–29, *27*, 37, 99g
Brown Berets 72
*Brown v. Board of Education* **71**

### C

Cabeza de Vaca, Álvar Núñez 9
California
    braceros in 37
    immigrants in 39
    labor strike in 68–69
    Latino organizations in 77–78, 79
    murals in *91*, 91–92
    school segregation in **71**
    Sleepy Lagoon Case in 20
    strike in 14
    zoot suit riots in 20–22, *21*
California Labor Relations Act 68–69
Carew, Rod 96
Caribbean
    Cuba *54*, 55–61, **58**, *60*
    Dominican Republic 61–63
Carter, Jimmy (U.S. president) **39**
Carter, Lynda 88
Casals, Rosemary 97
Castañeda, Carlos (Latino activist) **17**, 17–18
Castro, Fidel (Cuban dictator)
    Bay of Pigs and 58, **58**
    Cuban immigrants and 57
    in march *24*, 25
    Mariel boatlift and 59, 60
    rule of Cuba 56
Catholic Church 52–53
Caucasian Race Resolution 22
Central American immigrants 38–39
Cepeda, Orlando 96
Chávez, César (social activist) **28**, 28, 68–69
Chavez, Linda 83
Che Guevara, Ernesto (Cuban leader) 56
Chicago, Illinois 73
Chicana Rights Project 80
Chicano Film Festival 87
Chicano movement 66
children 69–73
Chiquita Banana 88
cinema. *See* film
citizenship, U.S. 45–46
civil rights
    Civil Rights Act 75–76
    Dolores Huerta and **68**
    education 69–73, **71**, 72m
    film industry and 86–87
    inspiration of Latino activists 67
    labor 67–69
    Latino movements/groups 65–67
    poem **92**
    of Puerto Ricans 45, 46, *70*, 73
    Victor Garcia at rally *64*, 65
Civil Rights Act 75–76
Clemente, Roberto 96
Cold War **26**, 58–59
Collazo, Oscar (independentista) 47
Colón, Miriam 90
colonia 99g
Columbus, Christopher 9
commonwealth 47
communism 25, **26**, 30–32, 99g
Community Service Organization 28, **28**
Concepción, Dave 96
Congressional Hispanic Caucus 80
Congressional Medal of Honor **15**, 16m, 32
conjunto music (*música norteña*) 94
constitution, Puerto Rico 47
Cordero, Andrés Figueroa (independentista) 48, *48*
Coronado, Francisco Vásquez de 9
Corrente, Arianne 1
*corrido* (ballad) 94
Cortés, Hernán 9
Cruz, Celia 95, *95*
Cuba
    baseball in 96
    Bay of Pigs 58, **58**
    communist Cuban leaders *24*, 25
    Fidel Castro's rule of 56–57
    Fulgencio Batista's rule of 55
    Mariel boatlift 59–61, *60*
    nuclear weapons in 58–59
Cuba, Joe 96
Cuban American Legal Defense and Education Fund 61
Cuban American National Council 61
culture, Latino
    art 90–92, *91*
    Culture Clash comedy group **84**, 85
    of immigrants 40–43, *42*
    literature **92**, 92–93
    Mexican 35
    movies **41**, 85–87, *86*

music 93–96, *95*
sports 96, 97
television 88–89
theater 89–90
Culture Clash comedy group *84*, 85

## D
De La Vega, James *8*, 9
De Soto, Hernando 9
democracy **26**, 30–32
Díaz, José 20
Didley, Bo 96
discrimination
    bracero program and 19
    Civil Rights Act and 75–76
    against Dominicans 63
    against Latinos 11, 13–14, 32
    against Mexican Americans 37–38
    against Puerto Ricans 50
    Sleepy Lagoon Case 20
    against war heroes 22–23, 94
    zoot suit riots 20–22, *21*
Dominican Republic 61–63
Dominicans 62–63
Domino, Fats 96

## E
Economic Opportunity Act (EOA) 76
education 37–38, 41, 69–73, **71**, 72*m*
Eisenhower, Dwight (U.S. president) 58
*El Diario/La Prensa* (newspaper) 66
*El Grito* (*The Shout*) magazine 92
*El Teatro Campesino* (the Farmworkers' Theater) 89–90
Elizondo, Hector 87
employment. *See* work
English language 69–70
Equal Employment Opportunity Commission 76
Estrada, Erik (Enrique) 88

## F
Fair Employment Practices Committee 17–18
family 36, 51–52
farm workers 14, 67–69, **68**. *See also* braceros
farming. *See* agriculture
Federal Alliance of Land Grants (*Alianza Federal de las Mercedes*) 66–67
Feliciano, José 96
film **41**, 85–87, *86*
Flores, Irving (independentista) *48*, 48

Florida
    bilingual education in 69–70
    Latino settlement in 10, 39, 56–57, 59, 63
    Mariel boatlift *60*, 60–61
football 97
Foraker Act 45, 99*g*
Frito Bandito 88

## G
García, Héctor (civil rights activist) 23
Garcia, Victor (civil rights activist) *64*, 65
G.I. Bill of Rights 20
G.I. Forum 66, 76–77
golf 97
Gonzalez, Richard "Pancho" 97
González, Rudolfo "Corky" **92**
Great Depression 11, 13–14
Great Migration **49**, 49–53
"green cards" 29
Guastella Film Producers 87
Guevara, Ernesto Che (communist Cuban leader) *24*, 25, 56
Gutiérrez, José Ángel (civil rights activist) 72, 82

## H
Harris, William W. 31–32
Hart-Celler Act 5–6, **6**
harvest of empire 4–5
*Harvest of Shame* (t.v. documentary) 26
hermandad 52, 99*g*
Hernández, Keith 96
Hispanic National Bar Association **79**
holidays 36, *44*, 45
hometown club 52
Honda, Mike (U.S. congressman) *74*, 75
Huerta, Dolores (social activist) 28, **68**, 68

## I
*I Am Joaquín/Yo Soy Joaquín* (González) **92**
*I Love Lucy* (television show) 41–42, *42*
illegal immigrants 32, 33. *See also* undocumented immigrants
immigrants
    assimilation pressure 40–42
    Central American 38–39
    Cuban *54*, 56–61, *60*
    culture of 40–43
    Mexican American 36–38, *37*
    new arrivals 35–36
    repatriation of 13
    South American 39–40
    undocumented 29–30
immigration
    Cuban *54*, 56–61, *60*
    Dominican 61–63
    Latino, history of 1–7, 10
    number of legal immigrants **29**
    Puerto Rican 18
    U.S. immigration policy 32–33
Immigration and Nationality Act 32–33
Immigration and Naturalization Service (INS) 27, 29, 30, **41**, 99*g*
independentista 47–48, *48*, 99*g*

## J
Japan 14, 15–16
Job Corps 76
jobs. *See* work
Jobs for Progress (SER) 76–77
Johnson, Lyndon B. (U.S. president) 5–6, 23, 59, 77
Juliá, Raúl 90

## K
KCOR-TV 42
Kennedy, John F. (U.S. president) 58–59, 79
King, Martin Luther, Jr. (civil rights activist) **67**, 67
Korean War 30–32, *31*

## L
*la Huelga* ("the Strike") 68
*La Opinión* (newspaper) 65
La Raza Unida Party (LRUP) 82–83
labor 67–69, **68**. *See also* work
Latin America
    Central American immigrants 38–39
    definition of 99*g*
    Latino immigration history 1–7
    South American immigrants 39–40
    U.S. interference in 25
Latinos. *See also* civil rights; culture, Latino; political power
    bracero program 18–19, *19*
    Central American immigrants 38–39
    challenges of 20–23, *21*
    culture of 40–43, **41**, *42*
    definition of 2–3
    in Great Depression 13–14
    histories of 6–7
    immigration to U.S. 4–6
    importance in U.S. 1–2
    Medal of Honor 16*m*
    Mexican Americans 36–38, *37*
    new arrivals 35–36
    Puerto Rican migration 45–53

South American immigrants 39–40
Spanish explorers and 8–9
United States and 9–10
in World War II *12*, **15**, 15–18, **17**
Latinos, in postwar society
  communist Cuban leaders march *24*, 25
  Korean War 30–32, *31*
  maquiladora program **33**
  undocumented immigrants 29–30
  U.S. immigration policy 32–33
  U.S. in Latin American affairs 25
  workers' rights 26–29, *27*, **28**
League of United Latin American Citizens (LULAC) 38, 66, **71**, 76–77, 86
Lebrón, Lolita (independentista) 48, *48*
literature, Latino **92**, 92–93
Little Havana, Florida 10, 57
Longoria, Félix (U.S. soldier) 22–23, 94
López, Nancy 97
Lopez, Trini 96
Los Angeles, California 1, 20–22, *21*
Los Angeles Chicano Cinema Coalition 87
Lozano, Ignacio E. 65
LRUP (La Raza Unida Party) 82–83

## M
magazine, Latino 43, 92
maquiladora program **33**
Marichal, Juan 96
Mariel boatlift 59–61, *60*
Marielitos *60*, 60–61
Marín, Luis Muñoz (governor of Puerto Rico) 46
Martinez, Joseph P. **15**
Méndez, Gonzalo **71**
*Méndez v. Westminster School District* **71**
mestizo 9, 99*g*
Mexican American Legal Defense and Education Fund (MALDEF) **79**, 80, 81, 86
Mexican American Political Association (MAPA) 78, *78*, 79
Mexican American Youth Organization (MAYO) 72–73
Mexican Americans
  civil rights of **71**, 72
  discrimination against 22–23
  immigrants 35–36
  life of 36–38, *37*
  repatriation of 11

Sleepy Lagoon Case 20
  in World War II 15, **15**
  zoot suit riots 20–22, *21*
Mexican Central League 96
Mexican-American War 10
Mexicans
  bracero program 18–19, *19*
  migrant family *34*
  number of legal Mexican immigrants **29**
  undocumented immigrants 29–30
  workers' rights 26–29, *27*, **28**
Mexico
  baseball in 96
  bracero program 18–19, *19*
  land lost to U.S. 3–4, 10
  maquiladora program **33**
  U.S. immigration policy and 32–33
Miami, Florida 56–57, 59
Midwest 35–36
migrant workers 69. *See also* braceros
migration 45, 49–53
Miranda, Rafael Canel *48*, 48
Mohr, Nicholasa 93
Montalbán, Ricardo 86–87, 88
Moreno, Rita 86, *86*, 87, 90
movies. *See* film
murals 90–92, *91*
music, Latino 93–96, *95*
*música norteña* (conjunto music) 94
mutual-aid societies 52

## N
National Association for the Advancement of Colored People (NAACP) **67**
National Farm Workers Association 68, **68**
neighborhood. *See* barrio
New Deal 13–14
New York 18, 49, **49**, 63
New York City, New York
  Central American immigrants in 39
  civil rights demonstration in *70*
  Puerto Ricans in 50–51, *51*
  South American immigrants in 40
  Spanish Harlem in *8*, 9, 10
newspapers, Latino 65–66
*Nilda* (Mohr) 93
North Korea 30–31
Northeast 40
NOSOTROS 86–87
nuclear weapons 58–59
Nuyoricans **49**

## O
Obledo, Mario G. (Latino activist) **79**
Oliva, Tony 96
Olmos, Edward James 87
Operation Bootstrap **47**
organizations, Latino
  American G.I. Forum 23
  in civil rights movement 65, 66–67, 72–73
  Cuban 61
  film industry and 86–87
  formation of 11
  political 77–81, *78*
  Puerto Rican 52
orquesta music 93
Ortiz, Carlos 97
Overmyer-Velázquez, Mark 1–7

## P
pachucos 21
Palomino, Ernesto 91
Pan American National Bank **82**
Panama Canal **39**
Pearl Harbor, Hawaii 14
Philippines 15–16
Piñero, Jésus T. (governor of Puerto Rico) 46
Piñero, Miguel 93
Pizarro, Francisco 9
Plunkett, Jim 97
poetry **92**, 92
Political Association of Spanish-Speaking Organizations (PASSO) 78, 79
political power
  Civil Rights Act 75–76
  Economic Opportunity Act 76
  La Raza Unida Party 81–83
  Latino political organizations 77–81, *78*
  Mario G. Obledo **79**
  Mike Honda **74**, 75
  Romana Acosta Bañuelos **82**
  SER 76–77
  VISTA **76**
  voting campaign *80*
prejudice. *See* discrimination
Principal, Victoria 88
Prinze, Freddie 88
protectorate 45
Puente, Tito *95*, 95
Puerto Rican Forum 52
Puerto Rican Traveling Theatre (PRTT) 90
Puerto Ricans
  at civil rights demonstration *70*
  Great Migration 49
  independentistas 47–48, *48*
  in Korean War *31*, 31–32

literature of 93
migration of 18
Nuyoricans **49**
Operation Bootstrap **47**
political resistance of 73
politics in Puerto Rico 46–47
in theater 90
as U.S. citizens 45–46
in World War II *12*, 13, 15
Puerto Rico 5, 45–53, **47**, 87

## Q
Quinn, Anthony 87

## R
racism 41–42, *42*. See also discrimination
Ramos, Armando 97
Reagan, Ronald (U.S. president) 83
religion 52–53
repatriate 99*g*
repatriation 11, 13, 30, **82**
Revueltas, Rosaura **41**
rights. See civil rights
riot 20–22, *21*, 73
Robinson, Jackie 96
Rodríguez, Patricia 92
Roosevelt, Franklin Delano (U.S. president) 13–14, 17, 46

## S
salsa 95
*Salt of the Earth* (film) **41**
San Antonio Cinefestival 87
Santa Fe Battalion 15
Santana, Carlos 96
school. See education
segregation 11, 22, 37–38, 66, 69, **71**
SER (Jobs for Progress) 76–77
*Sesame Street* (television show) 88–89
Sheen, Martin 87
*Short Eyes* (Piñero) 93
65th Infantry *31*, 31
Sleepy Lagoon Case 20
socialism 99*g*
South American immigrants 39–40
South Korea 30–31
Southwest 35, 36, 37–38, 67
Southwest Voter Registration and Education Project 80–81
Soviet Union 25, **26**, 30, 58–59
Spain 9–10, 55
Spanish explorers 9
Spanish Harlem (New York City, New York) *8*, 10, *44*, 50–51, *51*
Spanish International Network 89
Spanish language 69–72, 72*m*

Spanish-American War 5, 45
sports, Latinos in 85, 97
stereotypes 41–42, *42*, 85–87, 88
strike 14, 68, 99*g*

## T
television 41–42, *42*, 85, 88–89
*Temas* magazine 43
tennis 97
Texas
 discrimination in 19, 22–23
 LRUP work in 82
 political organization in 78, 79
 San Antonio Cinefestival in 87
 workers' rights in 26–27
theater, Latino 89–90
Tijerina, Reies López (Chicano activist) 67
time line, Latino-American fight for American values 98
Tinoco, Alberto 1
Torres, José Luis 97
Torresola, Griselio (independentista) 47
Treviño, Lee 97
Trujillo Molina, Rafael (Dominican Republic dictator) 62
Truman, Harry S. (U.S. president) 47

## U
undocumented immigrants 29–30, 32, 33, 62, 69
unions 14, 68–69
United Farm Workers 68
United States
 bilingual education legislation 72*m*
 Central American immigration to 38–39
 in Cold War **26**
 Cuba and 55, **58**, 58–59
 Cuban immigration to 59–61, *60*
 Dominican Republic immigrants 61–63
 immigration policy 32–33
 immigration to 1–7, **6**, **29**, 35–38
 in Korean War 30–32, *31*
 Latinos and 9–10
 Puerto Rico and 45–46
 in World War II 14–18, **15**, 16*m*
Unity Leagues 77
Univision 89
U.S. Census 2
U.S. Cuban Refugee Program 59
U.S. House of Representatives 48
U.S. military **15**, 15–16, 16*m*, *31*, 31–32

## V
Valdez, Luis 89
Valens, Richie 96
veterans, Latino 32
Viguié Film Productions 87
Volunteers in Service to America (VISTA) 76, **76**
voting *80*, 80–81
Voting Rights Act 81

## W
wages 18, 26–27, 50
Welch, Raquel 87
*West Side Story* (film) 86, *86*, 90
*Westminster School District, Méndez v.* **71**
wetbacks (*mojados*) 29
Wilson, Woodrow (U.S. president) 46
work
 affirmative action and 75–77
 after World War II 26
 bracero program for **18**, 18–19, *19*, 37
 of Dominicans 63
 fair labor, fight for 67–69, **68**
 in Great Depression 14
 Latino immigrant labor 6
 maquiladora program **33**
 Mexican farm laborer 1, *vi*
 Operation Bootstrap and **47**
 of Puerto Ricans 49, 50
 of undocumented immigrants 29–30
 in World War II 16–18, **17**
workers' rights, protection of 26–29, *27*, **28**
World War I 11, 46
World War II
 bracero program in **18**, 18–19, *19*
 discrimination and 22–23
 G.I. Bill of Rights 20
 Latinos on home front 16–18, **17**
 Latinos who fought in **15**, 15–16
 Medal of Honor 16*m*
 Puerto Ricans in *12*, 13, 46
 U.S. entry into 14

## Y
Ybor City, Florida 56, *57*
Young Lords 73

## Z
zoot suit riots 20–22, *21*

# About the Author

### Robin Doak

Robin Doak holds a B.A. in English, with a concentration in journalism, from the University of Connecticut. She has worked for Weekly Reader Corporation as an editor and is currently a freelance writer who, over the last 10 years, has authored and coauthored 38 books, primarily educational reading material for children.

### Mark Overmyer-Velázquez

Mark Overmyer-Velázquez, general editor and author of the preface included in each of the volumes, holds a BA in History and German Literature from the University of British Columbia, and MA, MPhil and PhDs in Latin American and Latino History from Yale University. While working on a new book project on the history of Mexican migration to the United States, he teaches undergraduate and graduate courses in Latin American and U.S. Latina/o history at the University of Connecticut.